WIDENING HORIZONS

WIDENING HORIZONS

Man's Quest to Understand
the Structure of the Universe

Zdeněk Kopal

Professor of Astronomy
University of Manchester

TAPLINGER PUBLISHING COMPANY

New York

First Published in the United States in 1971 by Taplinger
Publishing Co., Inc. New York, New York
Copyright © Zdeněk Kopal 1970

ISBN 0–8008–8320–9

Library of Congress Catalog Card Number 73–99307

Printed in the United States of America

'It is of great advantage that man should know his station, and not erroneously imagine that the whole Universe exists only for him.'

Maimonides (in Dalālat al-hā 'irin, Part III, Chapter XII; written around 1190 A.D.)

'The pleasure and delight of knowledge far surpasseth all other in Nature. We see in all other pleasures there is satiety; and after they be used, their verdure departeth, which showeth well that they be but deceits of pleasure, and not pleasures; and that it was the novelty which pleased, not the quality; and therefore we see that voluptuous men turn friars, and ambitious princes turn melancholy. But of knowledge there is no satiety, but satisfaction and appetite are perpetually interchangeable.'

Francis Bacon (1561–1626)

CONTENTS

1 Beginning of the Road

ASTRONOMY OF THE ANCIENTS

It will be the aim of the present little volume to outline for the general reader the course of the endless quest of man to recognise his position in the Universe around us by reasoning which could be based on astronomical observations. In doing so, we shall abstain from the obvious temptation to embellish our story with too many digressions in the domain of philosophy—which often places undue emphasis on the historical context of our subject—in an effort to trace all the sources whose eventual coalescence has resulted in the mighty stream of human science as we know it today.

We propose in our exposition to avail ourselves of the full benefit of hindsight, and single out—in historical retrospect—only those elements of our story which have proved to be permanent contributions to human science, and necessary stepping stones for its subsequent advances. To trace the process of gradual groping towards the truth—interesting as this might be from an historical point of view—would be too discursive for the main aim of our narrative. Instead, we intend to focus attention on the instances at which our astronomical ancestors—both distant and recent—arrived at the 'moments of truth', and were able to support their arguments by observations or reasoning, which not only convince them of the correctness of their arguments, but which we still find equally correct today.

To give an example of what we mean, and apply our thesis to the history of a sister-science, we should be quite unwilling to concede Democritos of Abdera (460–370 B.C.) his usual title of a father of the atomic theory of matter, merely on the grounds of his surmise—transmitted by tradition—that matter is not infinitely divisible. Clearly, any assertion of this type is either true or false—with an outright guess thus having a probability of one-half of being right—and Democritos may have expressed his view only in opposition to the contrary view then prevalent, in quest of originality. Needless to say, he did not (nor could he) adduce any rational arguments in favour of his view by which he could convince anyone of the correctness of his opinion—these were still almost two thousand years in the future.

With the beginnings of astronomy the situation was no different; nor are their sources easier to trace in time. There is no doubt that the early discoveries regarding the motion of the Sun and the Moon—the two most conspicuous celestial bodies in the sky— antedate the written history of mankind by centuries or millenia, and only megalithic monuments or other structures in stone bear mute witness to the proficiency of our neolithic ancestors in measuring the course of the time. Moreover, it was probably the recurrence of the principal celestial phenomena which first taught mankind that regularity exists in Nature. From the nomads who saw the morning star rise at dawn in the Chaldean plains or over the waters of the Pacific, to scientists who observe quasars or measure the velocities of recession of distant galaxies, the watchers of the sky have been foremost among those opening wider horizons to the inquisitive human mind.

The measurement of time with the aid of an appropriate lunar or solar calendar was no doubt stimulated by the needs of agriculture—to determine the advent of the seasons for sowing and harvest—as well as to fix the dates for the collection of taxes or religious festivals, and none of these tasks concerned as yet the position of man in relation to the celestial bodies around him. The first celestial object of inquisitive inquiry by awakening human intelligence was bound to be our own abode in the Universe—our Earth; and to trace the course of this inquiry will constitute the first legitimate objective of this book.

For a long time—centuries, millenia perhaps—such views as human beings in many parts of the world entertained about the astronomical position of their abode did not depart from the realm of speculative conjecture until the advent of the Greeks in the arena of human thought some time after 1000 B.C. To be sure, in the earliest literary monuments of Greece—that is to say, in the Homeric poems and the works of Hesiod—the Earth was still a flat circular disc. This was not stated explicitly, but only on this assumption could Poseidon from the mountains of Solym in Pisidia have seen Odysseus at Scheria on the further side of Greece, or Helios at his rising and setting watch his cattle on the island of Thrinakia. Around this flat disc, on the horizon, runs the river Oceanus, encircling the Earth and flowing back into itself. Over the flat Earth was the vault of heaven, covering it like a hemispherical dome; hence the Aethiopians dwelling in the extreme east and west were burned black by the Sun. Below the Earth was Tartarus, covered by the Earth and forming a kind of vault symmetrical with the heaven; Hades is supposed to be beneath the surface of the Earth, as far from the height of the heaven above as from the depth of Tartarus below (i.e., presumably in the hollow of the Earth's disc).

The dimensions of the heaven and Earth were only indirectly indicated; Hephaistos, cast down from Olympus, fell for a whole day till sundown before hitting the ground. On the other hand, according to Hesiod, an iron anvil would take nine days to pass from the heaven to the Earth, and nine days from Earth to Tartarus. The vault of heaven remained immovable for ever in one position; the Sun, Moon and stars moved around underneath it, rising from Oceanus in the east and plunging again into it in the west. What happened to the heavenly bodies after they set and before they rose again, the readers of Homer or Hesiod were not told. They could not have passed around under the Earth, because its underbelly— Tartarus—was never illuminated by the Sun. Possibly they were supposed to float around in Oceanus, past the north, till they reached the point of their rise in the east. But it was only subsequent Greek writers who represented Helios as sleeping at night, and being carried around by water on a golden bed or in a golden bowl.

This was but mythology of the nomadic age or of the beginnings of pastoral life, and the early Greek descriptions of it did not differ essentially from those current in other contemporary civilisations. However, not long following the time of Hesiod (the first half of the 8th century B.C.) the idea emerged which—for the first time in the history of mankind—raised the mythological speculations about the world around us to the rank of scientific cosmology: namely, a conjecture of the *spherical shape* of the Earth.

THE EARTH: Shape and Size

The conception that the Earth is a sphere was probably formulated by the Pythagorean school of pre-Socratic philosophy which flourished in southern Italy in the 5-6th century B.C. Tradition attributed it to Pythagoras himself (born at Samos about 570 B.C.) or Parmenides (born about 515 B.C.). Of extant sources it appeared first in Plato's dialogue *Phaidon*, where Socrates alluded (reputedly around 399 B.C.) to a controversy on the shape and size of the Earth in the following terms:

'I am convinced, then, . . . that if the Earth, being a sphere, is at the centre of the heavens, it has no need either of air or of any other such force to keep it from falling, but that the uniformity of the substance of the heaven in all its parts and the equilibrium of the Earth itself should suffice to hold it . . .'.

The idea of a spherical Earth we owe, therefore, to the Pythagoreans, and there is no indication that they would have borrowed it from any non-Greek source. If we are unwilling to grant to Pythagoras or Parmenides the undoubted priority of this discovery, it is for the same reason that we do not acknowledge Democritos as father of the atomic theory of matter: namely, that no discovery in the modern sense was made. For it is more than probable that the Pythagorean reasons behind their hypothesis of a spherical Earth were essentially aesthetic, and their doctrine may have run as follows: the most perfect shape of a solid is a sphere. The heavenly bodies are perfect, the Earth is a heavenly body, and, therefore, spherical. At least there is no indication whatsoever—contemporary or later—that the Pythagoreans had in mind anything else. What they did might possibly pass for philosophy, but not science as we understand this term today.

For the first scientific argument proving the Earth to be spherical we have to wait until the time of the great encyclopedist Aristotle (384–323 B.C.). In the books entitled *Meteorologica* and *De Coelo*, Aristotle stated that the Earth must be spherical because *the outline of the terrestrial shadow, cast on the disc of the Moon during lunar eclipses, is always circular*. Whether or not this argument—entirely sufficient to a modern mind as a proof of the proposition—was original with Aristotle, or whether Aristotle merely reported an opinion already formed, we do not unfortunately, know; for very little of the pre-

Aristotelian scientific literature has reached us. The same argument could have already been advanced by Anaxagoras (born about 499 B.C. at Clazomenae, died 428 B.C. at Lampsacos) the last great philosopher of the Ionian school, credited traditionally with the realization of the true nature of the lunar eclipses, and others have suggested Eudoxos of Cnidos (408–355 B.C.), a distinguished Ionian mathematician and astronomer, as a possible author of the proof.

To us—peering at the intellectual life of post-Socratic Greece through dim telescopes of research across a gulf of time of more than two thousand years—the full truth is unlikely ever to be known; but the possibility exists that, in *De Coelo*, Aristotle may have reported only the opinion which originated before his time. The fact remains, however, that the spherical form of the Earth was deduced from astronomical observations not later than by the middle of the third century before our era, by a geometrical argument whose validity has not been diminished by the ages which have elapsed since that time. Therefore, a knowledge that the Earth is a sphere has been in the intellectual possession of mankind for at least 2300 years.

Once we admit that the Earth is a sphere, the question is bound to be raised immediately: what is its size? As is invariably the case in the annals of science, quantitative determinations are always preceded by qualitative estimates. Thus Plato in his *Phaidon* makes Socrates say that . . . 'Moreover, I am convinced that the Earth is very great and that we, who live from the river Phasis as far as the Pillars of Heracles inhabit only a small part of it; like the ants of frogs around a pool, so we dwell around the (Mediterranean) sea; while there are many other men dwelling elsewhere in many regions of the same kind'.

The sense of this qualitative quotation indicates that, at any rate, Socrates and his contemporaries were aware that the size of the terrestrial globe was so large that the Mediterranean basin constituted only a very small part of it. The first specific figure describing the size of the Earth was given again by Aristotle (op. cit.) who quoted the circumference of the terrestrial globe to be 400 000 stades. The next estimate of the size of the Earth is found in Archimedes (287–212 B.C.) who declared that the circumference of the Earth was 3 000 000 stades long, or more; 'though some would

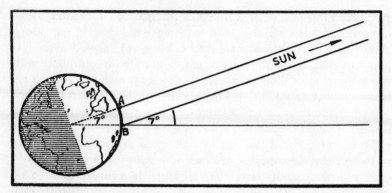

Fig. 1. The principle of the method by Eratosthenes for measuring the size of the Earth.

have it only 300 000'. The latter figure we find quoted again by Cleomedes (1st century B.C.) who mentioned anonymously a measurement in which the arc of the meridian between Syene (Aswan in Egypt) and Lysimachia (north of Gallipoli) was taken as one-fifteenth of the zodiac (i.e., 24°) and 20 000 stades long; so that, accordingly, the corresponding terrestrial circumference should come out close to 300 000 stades. The underlying data are, however, quite crude. The true difference in the latitudes of Lysimachia and Aswan being 16½°, and the two places are separated by 1800 kms (1118 mls). The estimate of 300 000 stades for the circumference of the Earth was also attributed (conjecturally) to Aristarchos (who flourished in the first half of the 3rd century B.C.); but most of our information really came to us from Cleomedes, who lived almost two hundred years later.

The most famous of the ancient attempts to measure the size of the Earth is undoubtedly that of Eratosthenes, born in the year of 276 B.C. in Cyrene, a great Alexandrian geographer who succeeded (around 240 B.C.) his master Kallimachos as director of the library in Alexandria, a position which he held until the time of his death in 194 B.C. Eratosthenes did not invent, but considerably perfected the method of his predecessors—namely, the double measurement of an arc of the meridian in degrees and in stades, by the introduction of new instruments for the measurement of the latitude (a gnomon, and skiotheron akin to a sundial); and for the measurement of distance he took also advantage of the royal surveys undertaken by the Egyptian government under Ptolemaios Euregetes. In most histories of science it is customary to quote Cleomedes' account of Eratosthenes' measurement of the arc from Syene to Alexandria at the time of the summer solstice (when the Sun stands overhead at Aswan of 14° northern latitude, while reaching at altitude 7° short of the zenith at Alexandria, situated approximately the same meridian). But other sources suggest that Eratosthenes may have undertaken several other measurements before reaching his final estimate of 252 000 stades for the length of the Earth's circumference.

The ancient world accepted Eratosthenes' measurements as the best possible one; the method was sound, and the data could scarcely be improved (they actually were not until the 17th century). For the sake of completeness we should, however, at least mention another estimate of the circumference of the Earth, credited to the Stoic philosopher Poseidonios (2nd–1st century B.C.) and reportedly based on the arc between Alexandria and Rhodes. Two versions of his results have come down to us: according to Cleomedes, Poseidonios' result for the length of the circumference was 240 000 stades, while according to Strabo, only 180 000 stades. Hipparchos—the greatest astronomer of antiquity—had apparently accepted Eratosthenes' value quoted above —but Claudius Ptolemy, author of the famous *Almagest*. who followed Hipparchos otherwise so closely in his mathematics and astronomy, adopted nevertheless the circumference of the Earth as 180 000 stades in his *Geography*, thereby giving it a prestige that rivalled that of the value of Eratosthenes.

Is it possible that the ancient ideas as to the size of the Earth could have been as vague and uncertain as a comparison of the two values of 180 000 and 252 000 might lead one to infer? Scarcely so, for the difference widely exceeds the limits of observational errors affecting the ancient measurements. The reason is to be sought, primarily, in the vexing question of the calibration and intercomparison of the ancient units of length. For it is a fact— attested amply by non-astronomical evidence—that the Greek stade was a variable quantity, and in particular instances almost always uncertain. For centralization and standardization was impossible under the political disunity of ancient Greece. The Persian or the Roman Empires might impose their single standards far and wide, but among the Greek cities several standards were used at the same time. The Roman mile of 5000 feet corresponds to a constant value of about 1488 metres or 0.9248 of our statute mile; but for the Greek stade ancient sources give several values ranging from $7\frac{1}{3}$ to 10 stades to a Roman mile. The only (though indirect) evidence on the length of the Eratosthenes' stade is a solitary—but apparently reliable—statement by Plinius, to the effect that 'schoenus patet Eratosthenis ratione stadia XI'. Now 'schoenus' was an Egyptian measure of length, which the Egyptologists (on the basis of measurements of the pyramids and other archeological evidence) have long maintained to be about 0.525 of a metre (21"). On this basis Eratosthenes' value for the length of the equator of the terrestrial globe would be 6300 schoeni or 39 690 km (24 662 mls)—as compared with the actual mean circumference of 40 120 km (24 929 mls). On this theory, Eratosthenes' results would be very near the truth; so near, in fact, as to make us suspect it to be partly accidental; but the length of the stade underlying its computation (i.e., 9.45 to a Roman mile) is irrational and not known from anywhere else. An alternative reduction of Eratosthenes' value has been undertaken on the assumption that the actual value of the schoenus (based on different historical evidence) was such as to lead, in the light of Pliny's quotation given above, to 10 stades to a Roman mile, which would render Eratosthenes' determination of the Earth's circumference to be 25 200 Roman miles, or 37 500 kms (23 301 mls); and although this result errs more than the previous one, it is perhaps more probable of the two on historical grounds; for a stade of 10 to a mile is not otherwise unknown.

Evidence of the length of the stade used in other ancient measurements of the dimensions of the Earth is, therefore, not unambiguous. However, there may be a partial solution of the discrepancy between the values ascribed to Eratosthenes and Poseidonios—a solution which would also support the view that Eratosthenes used a stade of 10 to a mile. In later times, at least the common stade was that of $7\frac{1}{2}$ to a mile. Now $10:7\frac{1}{2}=4:3=240\ 000:180\ 000$. If we assume that the lower Poseidonian number represents merely a conversion from one standard to another, the contradiction is liquidated and a stade of one-tenth of a Roman mile should be used to convert both the 240 000 (Poseidonios) and 252 000 (Eratosthenes) values to kms. Thus the two outstanding ancient estimates of the size of the Earth—that by Eratosthenes and Ptolemy (Poseidonios)—can then be brought into a virtual agreement, and reveal that the length of the circumference should be between 37 500 and 35 600 kms (23 301 and 22 121 mls). Now the actual length of this circumference is known to be 40 120 kms (24 929 mls), from which it transpires that the ancient determinations erred by a defect of 6.5% (Eratosthenes), or, at most, 11% (Poseidonios).

The reader will, I hope, forgive this somewhat technical digression into ancient metrology, but its result was worth the trouble; for it provides virtual assurance that, notwithstanding rather crude techniques for measurement of both arcs and lengths on the surface of the Earth, ancient geometers did sufficiently well in their task to provide posterity with a very realistic approximation of the actual size of our Earth. In fact, as far as the general features are concerned, subsequent ages were but to confirm and refine by a few per cent the facts first learned by the Greeks during the efflorescence of hellenistic culture, centered on Alexandria, in the second and third centuries before Christ. For the next two thousand years there was no progress, and the ancient traditions got garbled by transmission to such an extent that Christopher Columbus set out in 1492 A.D. on his transatlantic voyage with the firm belief in the Poseidonian value for the length of the terrestrial circumference, reduced to the medieval units by use of a wrong conversion factor which made the Earth smaller by a full quarter of its actual size.

THE SUN AND THE MOON

A realistic determination of the physical size of our terrestrial abode provided the Greek scholars with the requisite means for deeper penetration into space on the wings of their thoughts; and the sequel was not slow to unroll. The next step—to fathom the size and distance of the two other most conspicuous celestial bodies, the Sun and the Moon—was already taken, in fact, before the time of Eratosthenes, and its hero was Aristarchos of Samos (to distinguish him by his full name from Aristarchos of Samothrace, the philologist)—a great name in the history of science, shining like a beacon across the intervening gulf of time.

Just when he was born, we do not know—probably around 310 B.C.; and in his youth he was probably a pupil of the physicist Strato of Lampsacos in Athens. The only fixed date in the life of Aristarchos is the year of 281 B.C., when he observed (according to Hipparchos) the time of the summer solstice—an observation later used by Hipparchos (2nd century B.C.). We know that he was calumnied for the boldness of his view by the stoic philosopher Kleanthes some time after 264 B.C., and quoted by Archimedes in the *Sand-Reckoner* before 216 B.C. We do not, however, know where he lived—whether in Athens or Alexandria—nor when he died; but the most part of his life was probably spent in the first half of the 3rd century B.C.

The only one of his works to reach our time is a little tract entitled *On the Sizes and Distances of the Sun and the Moon*, and this alone would be sufficient to earn its author scientific immortality. Its contents and form illustrate well many peculiar aspects of Greek science, as well as the genius of its author. Following the style of Euclid's work on geometry, the tract of Aristarchos consists of a series of eighteen geometrical propositions, preceded by six 'hypotheses' which lay down the observational basis of the whole discussion.

Of these, hypotheses (1) and (3) 'that the Moon receives its light from the Sun, and that, at the time of the Half Moon (i.e., first or last quarter) the great circle dividing the bright and dark portions of the lunar globe lies in the line of sight' go back, in fact, to Anaxagoras (if not to Thales) and provide only the necessary background. The actual gist of the contribution made by Aristarchos rests in his 'hypothesis' that (4) 'At the time of Half Moon, the Moon's (angular) distance from the Sun is less than a quadrant by one-thirtieth of a quadrant (i.e., equal to 87°), and that (5) 'The width of the Earth's shadow (at the distance where the Moon passes through it during eclipse) is that of two Moons'.

The last (sixth) 'hypothesis', asserting that 'The (apparent diameter of the) Moon subtends (in the sky the angle of) one-fifteenth of a sign of the zodiac', is superfluous for a part of the argument and the weakest of them all; for the 'signs of the zodiac' (Aries, Taurus . . . Amphora, Pisces) being twelve in number, each was supposed to extend over one-twelfth of a circle (i.e., 30°); one one-fifteenth of it would have made the apparent diameter of the

Moon as large as $2°$, while it is actually no larger than $\frac{1}{2}°$. We do not know how to explain so gross an over-estimate except, possibly, as a copying error, for this younger contemporary—the great mathematician Archimedes of Syracuse (287–212 B.C.)—in his writings credited Aristarchos with a knowledge that the apparent diameters of the Sun and Moon were a $\frac{1}{720}$ th part of the entire zodiac (i.e., half a degree); so that if the earlier value of $2°$ was not an error introduced in the text by a subsequent copyist, Aristarchos himself realised the over-estimate soon after the original text was written.

But (as the matter is really irrelevant to the subject proper) let us see what Aristarchos deduced from his hypotheses (4) and (5) which are central to his thesis. If (4) were true, it would follow immediately (see Figure 2) that the (topocentric) distance D to the Moon should bear to the distance $D_\odot$ of the Sun the ratio equal to $\cot 87° = 0.0524\ldots$, rendering the Sun nine times as far from the observer as the Moon. Since, moreover, both the Sun and the Moon appear in the sky to exhibit discs of approximately the same angular diameter, it would follow that the Sun should in reality be 19 times larger than the Moon.

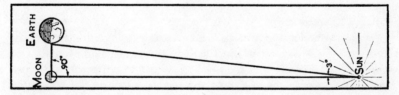

Fig. 2. The principle of the method of Aristarchos for measuring the distance to the Sun.

What should be the relative dimensions of the Earth in this system, and the distance between the Earth and the Moon expressed in terms of the size of the terrestrial globe? The answer should be provided by the hypothesis (5) according to which the section of the terrestrial shadow cone (tangent to the Sun and the Earth) should, at the Moon's distance, be twice as large as a cross-section of the Moon; and, therefore, its diameter should be $\frac{2}{19}$ times that of the Sun. Let, in what follows, $r_\odot$, $r_\oplus$ denote the radii of the Sun and of the Earth, respectively, while $D_\odot$ and $D_{\mathbb{C}}$ stand for the geocentric distances of the Sun and the Moon. If so, it follows from the similarity of the right-angle triangles on Figure 2 that

$$\frac{r_\odot - r_\oplus}{D_\odot} = \frac{r_\oplus - \frac{2}{19}r_\odot}{D_\mathbb{C}}, \tag{1}$$

which for

$$\frac{D_\odot}{D_\mathbb{C}} = \tan 87° = 19 \tag{2}$$

leads to the ratio

$$\frac{r_\odot}{r_\oplus} = \frac{1 + \dfrac{D_\odot}{D_\mathbb{C}}}{1 + \dfrac{2}{19}\dfrac{D_\odot}{D_\mathbb{C}}} = \frac{20}{3}. \tag{3}$$

Accordingly, the Sun should be $6\frac{2}{3}$ times as large as the Earth; and the Moon,

$$\frac{20}{3}\left(\frac{1}{19}\right) = \frac{20}{57} \tag{4}$$

or 0.35 times as large.

It is only when we turn to the evaluation of the distance of the Sun and the Moon from the Earth in terms of the dimensions of the terrestrial globe that we need to appeal to Aristarchos' 'hypothesis (6)' stating the apparent angular diameter of the Moon (or the Sun) to be 2°. With a semi-diameter of 1° the distance to the Moon would result as

$$D_\mathbb{C} = \frac{20}{57}\left(\frac{180°}{\pi}\right)r_\oplus = 20.1\ r_\oplus \tag{5}$$

and that to the Sun,

$$D_\odot = 19D_\mathbb{C} = 382\ r_\oplus. \tag{6}$$

It may be added here that, subsequently, these results were refined by Hipparchos (2nd half of the 2nd century B.C.) who is reported to have estimated (apparently from the duration of the total phase of lunar eclipses) the size of the cross-section of the terrestrial shadow-cone at the distance of the Moon to be more correctly, 8/3 times that of the Earth—a result leading to an improved value of the ratio

$$\frac{r_{\mathbb{C}}}{r_{\oplus}} = \frac{3}{11}\left(1 + \frac{D_{\mathbb{C}}}{D_{\odot}}\right), \tag{7}$$

replacing (4). Since, moreover, Aristarchos himself later reduced the apparent angular diameter of the Sun and the Moon to $\frac{1}{2}^{\circ}$, the corresponding distance to the Moon resulted as

$$D_{\mathbb{C}} = \frac{3}{11}\left\{\left(\frac{180^{\circ}}{\pi}\right) \div \frac{1^{\circ}}{4}\right\}\left(1 + \frac{D_{\mathbb{C}}}{D_{\odot}}\right)r_{\oplus} \tag{8}$$

$$= 62\left(1 + \frac{D_{\mathbb{C}}}{D_{\odot}}\right)r_{\odot}$$

superseding equation (5).

As to the ratio $D_{\odot}/D_{\mathbb{C}}$, Hipparchos considered its value to lie between 20 and 30 (making the Sun 20–30 times as far from us as the Moon)—still a hopeless underestimate. However, as it entered the right-hand sides of equation (7) or (8) only through the reciprocal,* its inaccuracy made but little difference to Hipparchos' conclusion that the lunar globe is only 0.28 times as large as the Earth in size (the modern value of this ratio being 0.2728); and that the distance separating us from the Moon was but little larger than 62 terrestrial radii—the correct value of which is now known to oscillate monthly (on account of the eccentricity of the lunar relative orbit around the Earth) between 57.20 and 63.84! As, moreover, the absolute dimensions of the terrestrial globe were, at that time, known (through the preceding work of Eratosthenes) within some 4% of their actual value, it follows that the absolute size and separation of the components of the Earth-Moon system were known to our astronomical ancestors correctly within a few per cent since the second century before our era—certainly no mean achievement!

* Ignoring it we should merely replace a convergent shadow cone cast by the Earth into space by a cylinder of terrestrial cross-section.

With the Sun it was still a very different story. But before we turn our attention to it let us pause briefly to appreciate the achievements already accomplished. In the work of Aristarchos, which originated probably sometime between 280–260 B.C., we meet for the first time in the history of astronomy a method for direct determination of the distances of celestial bodies from observational data, and the notion resulting from it that the Sun is about nineteen times more distant than the Moon lingered in astronomy for the better part of the subsequent 2000 years.

The form in which this result was obtained underwent, to be sure, a long evolution and was very different from that presented in the preceding paragraphs. Today, the underlying geometry can be easily handled by a schoolboy. Not so at the time of Aristarchos, who had as yet no inkling of what is familiar to us under the term of 'trigonometric functions', and although the Greeks of his time already knew the concept of 'irrational numbers', they never used them in astronomy. Instead, the entire discussion in Aristarchos' tract is carried out in terms of rational fractions, and all results expressed carefully in terms of fractions 'larger than' and 'smaller than' the desired quantity. For instance, the value of the ratio $r_\odot/r_\oplus$ as given by our equation (3) and involving the crucial quantity $D_\odot/D_\text{\text(} = \tan 87° = 19.081 \ldots$ was approximated as lying between $\frac{19}{3}$ and $\frac{43}{6}$; and similarly with other results. To accomplish this, and comprise each result within the limits of sufficiently close inequalities given by rational fractions, called for a considerable degree of mathematical skill in which the Greeks excelled—much more so, in truth, than in the domain of astronomical observations.

The basic observational data which were necessary for the theory of Aristarchos to furnish any concrete results were his postulates (4)—(6); but note that he did not call them 'observations', but 'hypotheses', and nothing whatever was said on the way in which these may have been arrived at. This can be understood only if we realise that Greek scholars like Aristarchos were primarily mathematicians rather than astronomers, and that celestial bodies just happened to become the objects of their geometrical problems, the precise value of the observed quantities entering it was not very important for the sake of exposition.

To give the observers their due, Aristarchos' estimate of the size of the cross-section of the terrestrial shadow at the distance of the

Moon—making it twice the size of the Moon itself—was not too bad, and Hipparchos' subsequent estimate increasing the factor 2 to $\frac{8}{3}$ proved to be remarkably accurate. However, the crucial angle of 87° between the Sun and the Moon at first quarter was a gross underestimate (its actual value differing only by 9′ from 90°); though Aristarchos or his contemporaries could scarcely be expected to do much better, for their observations would have been hopelessly vitiated by refraction of light in our atmosphere (the effect of which on astronomical observations appears not to have been realised before the time of Ptolemy in the first half of the second century A.D.); and the timing of the lunar first quarter would have to be accurate within thirty seconds of time to get the other angles of the triangle on Figure 2 correctly within one minute of arc—an obvious impossibility even with the aid of a telescope today.

In other words, while the geometrical methods proposed by Aristarchos and Hipparchos were quite adequate to deal with the mensuration of the Earth-Moon system, and furnish reasonable results on the basis of observations that could be made in antiquity, they were unable to do so properly for the Sun—which, as we now know, is not 19 times, but 400 times as far from us as the Moon. Therefore, the dimensions of the Sun were likewise hopelessly underestimated in antiquity. But it was realised clearly by Aristarchos, on the basis of the arguments presented in this section, that of the three bodies—the Sun, Moon and the Earth—the Sun must be by far the largest. This was indeed a major—though as yet inadequate—step forward from the time (only some 160 years before the time of Aristarchos) when (according to Diogenes Laertios) the Athenian mob banished Anaxagoras into exile for subversive activities, which included the teaching that the Sun was a fiery stone, larger in size than the peninsula of Peloponnesos.

A comparison of the radii of the Sun and the Earth does not, perhaps, speak as eloquently as a comparison of their respective volumes. When Aristarchos said, in his tract, that 'The Sun stands to the Earth in a ratio larger than 6859/27 but smaller than 79507/216', he meant that the volume of the Sun must be between 254 and 368 times the volume of the Earth. Possibly it was this gross disparity and the enormous bulk of the Sun, apparent already at that time, which suggested to Aristarchos the idea that it was not proper for a body so large to revolve around the much smaller Earth but that, on the contrary, it should reside itself at the centre. Whatever were his reasons, we do not know, but we possess sufficient evidence to show that, some time after the completion of his tract on *The Size and Distances of the Sun and the Moon*, Aristarchos also conceived—for the first time in the history of mankind—the idea of a *heliocentric* planetary system, which we shall now proceed to describe.

THE SOLAR SYSTEM

The Sun and the Moon are the brightest celestial objects seen in the sky, and the only ones exhibiting discs of finite angular diameter to the naked eye. They were, however, not the only denizens of the heavens to have attracted the attention of men since time immemorial. The stars themselves—light points attached to the celestial sphere—showed no indication of any motion other than their diurnal nightly course from East to West, thought to be due to a rotation of their entire sphere—but five 'wandering stars', or planets, were discovered in the course of time, three of which (Venus, Mars and Jupiter) were brighter at times than any 'fixed' star, and all of which appeared to follow motions which were quite complicated. In particular, while the two 'inner planets'—Mercury and Venus—never departed too far from the Sun and preceded or followed it in the sky before sunrise or after sunset, the 'outer planets'—Mars, Jupiter and Saturn—described each year characteristic loops in the sky, whose representation provided the Greek mathematicians and philosophers with the first major 'astronomical problem'.

Looking back at this stage in the development of our science from a retrospect of more than 2500 years, we wish that at least the speculative philosophers had kept out of it; for the false seed which some of them planted in the human mind at that time proved singularly disastrous for the future progress of science, and stood in the way of real understanding of the mechanics of the solar system till the beginning of the 17th century of our era: namely, their mistaken a priori assertion that *the motions of all celestial bodies must be circular and uniform*. There was, to be sure, never a shred of valid evidence for this kind of 'epistemological trash', which goes back no doubt to the Pythagoreans, and must have been initially advanced only by its aesthetic appeal. But once it took root, what an effort it required to shake it off!

The shortcomings of a world system based on such premises must have become manifest from the very beginning, for none of the planets move uniformly along a circular path to any approximation. This fact, unfortunately, brought also the worst out of the theoreticians; for rather than give up a preconceived wrong idea, our philosophers and mathematicians in their wake embarked, instead, on a series of rescue operations which well documented the popular saying that there was 'a method in their madness'. The less reasonable their arguments became, in retrospect, from the physical point of view, the more mathematical ingenuity they employed to buttress their unlikely concepts. Although, today, we cannot but deplore these lamentable twists and turns in the gradual evolution of astronomical science, the reader may understand, I hope, that our aim is also to attempt to drive home a historical lesson; for aren't we, perchance, guilty of similar intellectual eccentricities in (say) theoretical nuclear or particle physics today? How many of our cherished axioms may be similarly unsound and may one day have to be relegated to the same wastepaper basket as the 'epistemological trash' of the Pythagoreans?

It is indeed instructive to follow in retrospect the methods which the Greek mathematicians employed to 'save the phenomena' and reconcile the observed movements of the planets with the Pythagorean conception of uniform circular motion. If a simple circular model would not do, the only way out would seem to be to superpose more than one uniform and circular motion on each other. If the planets did not move uniformly along the arc of a circle (and no observer could have ever been under the illusion that they did), perhaps the planet moves so along a subsidiary circle whose centre describes, in turn, uniformly another circle; or three or more motions may be so combined in order to 'save the phenomena' or, rather, a theory resting on entirely arbitrary assumptions.

The commencement of this geometrical merry-go-round may be traced to Eudoxos (408–355 B.C.) and his theory of homocentric spheres—in fact, he needed twenty-seven of them (one for the stars, three for the Sun and the Moon each; while each of the five planets required four—each turning around a different axis and

27

with different speed) to 'save the phenomena' with sufficient approximation. Hipparchos (second half of the 2nd century B.C.) and Ptolemy (first half of the 2nd century A.D.) added more; and using the geometrical theory of epicycles laid down by Apollonios in the second half of the 3rd century B.C., also displaced the Earth from the centre of their circles to gain additional degrees of freedom.

But, to the eternal glory of Greek science, at least one of their mathematicians saw the planetary theory in a different light— Aristarchos of Samos, whose treatise (probably a juvenile work) on *The Size and Distance of the Sun and the Moon* we discussed in the preceding section. It is the only work of his which reached us in its completeness; yet, however important a landmark this treatise proves to be in the history of our subject, its importance is overshadowed by another contribution by Aristarchos which may have remained unwritten or—what was written—was lost; so that we know about it only by hearsay and references by his contemporaries. Thus from Plutarch (*De Facie in Orbe Lunae*) we learn that Aristarchos was threatened by Kleanthes of Assos (head of the Athenian Stoa between 264-232 B.C.) with a lawsuit for impiety, 'for moving the hearth of the universe and trying to save the phenomena by the assumption that the heaven is at rest, but that the Earth revolves in an oblique orbit, while rotating around its own axis'.

References like these make us wonder about, say, the fate of Charles Darwin, if his works had been completely lost, and all that had been handed down to posterity on his theory of evolution were a few fragments of the sermons about him by Bishop Wilberforce. But—fortunately for Aristarchos and ourselves—we have, in addition, an almost contemporary testimony recorded by the great mathematician Archimedes (287–212 B.C.) in his famous book *Psammites* (Sand-Reckoner)—words which no one can read without emotion remembering that they were written before 216 B.C.

'You [King Gelon II, tyrant of Syracuse, who died before 216 B.C.] are aware that universe (Κοσμος) is the name given by most astronomers to the sphere whose centre is the centre of the Earth, and whose radius is equal to the distance between the centre of the Sun and the centre of the Earth. This is the common account as you have heard from astronomers. But Aristarchos of Samos brought out a book consisting of some hypotheses [of the meaning of 'hypothesis' in this connection, cf. the preceding section] wherein it appears, as a consequence of assumptions made, that the (real) universe is many times greater than the one just mentioned. His hypotheses are that fixed stars and the Sun remain unmoved, that the Earth revolves about the Sun in the circumference of a circle, the Sun lying in the middle of the orbit, and that the sphere of the fixed stars, situated about the same centre as the Sun, is so great that the circle in which he supposes the Earth to revolve bears such a proportion to the distance of the fixed stars as the centre of the sphere bears to its surface . . . (by which) we must take Aristarchos to mean this: since we conceive the Earth to be, so to speak, the centre of the Universe, the ratio which the Earth bears to what we describe as the 'Universe' is equal to the ratio which the sphere containing the circle in which he supposes the Earth to revolve, bears to the sphere of the fixed stars'.

Considering the time at which this passage was written, its contents are stupendous, and would be almost incredible if we had it from any other source. But we have no reason to doubt Archimedes, who was born within the lifetime of Aristarchos, and might have known him personally.

To paraphrase the above passage, in plainer words, Aristarchos of Samos, who lived in the first half of the 3rd century B.C., placed the centre of the Universe in the Sun (instead of the Earth), and set out to 'save the phenomena' by postulating the daily rotation of the Earth about its own axis, as well as the yearly rotation of the Earth around the Sun. According to him, all the planets circle around the Sun—except for the Moon which alone revolves around the Earth (as attested by the phases which it exhibits in the course of a month). The positions of the stars are fixed for Aristarchos, and their motion at night is only apparent, arising as it does naturally from the daily rotation of the Earth, about its own axis, in the opposite direction.

In postulating this daily motion Aristarchos was not entirely original, for the same hypothesis was previously advanced by Heracleides of Pontos (born after 388 B.C., died between 315–310 B.C.), whose ideas ascribing to the Earth one (the rotational) motion, and allowing at least the inner planets—Mercury and Venus—to revolve around the Sun, contained an anticipation of the model of the solar system developed by Tycho Brahe eighteen centuries later. But the idea of the second motion of the Earth—its revolution around the Sun—was conceived by Aristarchos without, apparently, the benefit of any predecessors; and it proved to be the more fertile of the two; for it explained, in a natural manner, all the retrograde loops exhibited by the outer planets as the mere reflex of our own yearly terrestrial motion around the Sun, without the need for any elaborate epicycles or eccentric spheres.

Moreover, the sphere of the fixed stars is, according to Aristarchos, so immense that the dimensions of the Earth's entire orbit around the Sun shrink into insignificance in comparison with the distance of the stars. This last 'hypothesis' is the most astonishing of all—coming down to us, as it does, from the middle of the third century B.C.—for it implies a vast expansion of the size of the Universe from the views prevalent at that time. The modern reader will easily grasp why it was necessary for Aristarchos to make this postulate: namely, because of an effective absence of a yearly parallax of the fixed stars (see Chapter IV). The geocentric picture of the world, prevalent up to that time, left the dimensions of the Universe completely outside the confines of rational determination, and wholly within the domain of speculative thought. However, once the Sun was made to replace the Earth as the centre of the Universe, it must have occurred to Aristarchos that the dimensions of the terrestrial orbit around the Sun offer a much larger baseline for triangulation of cosmic distances—in much the same way as he himself previously used the dimensions of our terrestrial globe to triangulate the relative dimensions of the Earth-Moon system and of the Sun. Moreover, while—on the geocentric view—the planetary epicycles represented merely arbitrary geometrical characteristics, necessary to account for the observed motions of the 'wandering stars'; on the heliocentric hypothesis the angular dimensions of these epicycles (representing then a reflex of the terrestrial motion in an orbit of given size) provided a logical tool for setting up an orderly model of the entire solar system, and expressing the dimensions of the planetary orbits in terms of the Earth-Sun distance taken as a unit.

Whether or not Aristarchos actually carried out these computations, and thus constructed the first actual model of the solar system as it was known to the ancients, we do not, unfortunately, know; for his book to which Archimedes referred is irretrievably lost, and no account of it reached us other than in the quotation listed above. He could have, however, done so; and Archimedes's account makes it clear at least that Aristarchos was aware of the smallness of the 'parallax' of fixed stars, and not only realised, but accepted, its far-reaching implications. For a star (or any other celestial object) situated at a finite distance from us should be seen in different directions in the sky at different times of the year—as the position of the terrestrial observer changes in space—the result being that the place of such a body should yearly describe in the sky a so-called 'parallactic ellipse", which should become a circle for objects seen in a direction normal to the plane in which the Earth moves (the so-called 'ecliptic'), and degenerate into a straight-line motion for objects in the plane of the ecliptic. But whatever the position of the star may be with respect to the ecliptic, the amplitude of its parallactic motion (i.e., the so-called parallax π) should be a measure of its distance from us, expressed in terms of the length of the baseline of our observations. As, moreover, the dimensions of the terrestrial orbit are much larger than those of the Earth itself, observations made at different times of the year could be used to triangulate much greater distances in space than could be done from the Earth alone.

The foregoing quotation from Archimedes makes it obvious that Aristarchos was aware of this situation, as well as of the fact that fixed stars showed no measurable parallax—a fact which, on his heliocentric hypothesis, meant that the dimensions of the 'eighth sphere' of the stars must be stupendous. Just how large they should be follows from the well-known expression for the parallax,

$$\pi = 206\,265\,(D_\odot/D_*) \text{ seconds of arc,} \qquad (9)$$

where $D_\odot$ denotes, as before, the Earth-Sun distance (which we now call one 'astronomical unit'); and D_*, the distance to the stars. Now the angular measurements of the Greeks were not precise enough to enable them to detect parallactic motions in the sky smaller than (approximately) $10' = 600''$ of arc. Since, however, according to a previous work of Aristarchos (cf., equation 6) $D_\odot = 382\,r_\oplus$, it would follow from (9) that

$$D_* \; \rangle \; 343 D_\odot \sim 1.31 \times 10^5\,r_\oplus.$$

Moreover, as the absolute value of $r_\oplus$ was (cf. Section 2) at that time already known to be close to 6700 km (4163 mls), it follows that the minimum distance to the stars on Aristarchos' hypothesis would have been about 5.21 (3.24 mls) $\times$ 10^9 km, or approximately the distance at which we know now that the planet Pluto revolves around the Sun, marking the outer limit of the solar system.

Today, astronomers would not even wince at such a distance; but to the contemporaries of Aristarchos it must have appeared incomprehensively large—so large as to defy imagination. As a result, it evoked but little response at that time. That it was apparently ridiculed by philosophers should surprise no one who recalls the reaction of the Christian religions—catholic or protestant—to Copernicus and his followers in more recent times. Archimedes—one of the greatest scientific spirits of antiquity—was open-minded, but plainly noncommittal; and of other scientists of that age, only Seleucus of Chaldea seems to have accepted Aristarchos' heliocentric system as his own.

Historians of science—Georges Sarton, for instance—have criticized Hipparchos (second half of the 2nd century B.C.), the greatest astronomer of antiquity, for 'extreme conservatism and timidity of his mind (which) prevented him from rejecting the geocentrical system, for the long predominance of which he is chiefly responsible'; although it was Ptolemy (living in the first half of the second century A.D.) rather than Hipparchos, who was chiefly responsible for its perpetuation. Even though paucity of sources make it well-nigh impossible to trace the whole story (of all the works of Hipparchos, only one—an apparently juvenile fragment—has been preserved from antiquity; all else we know about him has reached us indirectly), it is perhaps not difficult to see the reasons which may have made it impossible for him to embrace the heliocentric system: namely, that it failed to represent the observations (to 'save the phenomena') within the limits of observational errors of his time. It should be kept in mind that—unlike Eudoxos or Aristarchos—Hipparchos was not a philosopher interested mainly in the mathematical aspects of the problem (although he did much to develop the formal theory of the epicycles), but rather in the critical combination of observations by which he earned his greatest triumphs, such as the discovery of the precession of the equinoxes.

As such, Hipparchos could not have failed to notice that the heliocentric system—although geometrically simpler—could not represent the observed motions of celestial bodies really any better than the earlier geocentric one, and especially for Mars the differences between theory and observations would amount to whole degrees of arc. Discrepancies of this magnitude would have been intolerable to Hipparchos who was, in fact, a forerunner and kindred spirit of astronomers like Bradley or Bessel of more modern times; and to such men the verdict of the observations would matter (rightly) much more than formal simplicity or theoretical logic.

In point of fact, the heliocentric system of Aristarchos constituted only one step necessary for the proper understanding of the mechanics of the solar system. The other necessity was to give up the Pythagorean pre-conceptions regarding the uniformity of circular motions of celestial bodies, and there is no indication that Aristarchos ever contemplated so radical a departure from tradition. We know, in retrospect, that Copernicus in the 16th century of our era had to resort to a graft of all the paraphernalia of the Ptolemaic epicycles onto the heliocentric system of Aristarchos to 'save the phenomena' and account for the observed planetary positions at least within 10 minutes of arc. The real simplicity of the solar system in its full grandeur did not become manifest until Johannes Kepler in the first decade of the 17th century broke at last the spell of the Pythagorean preconceptions and recognised the planetary orbits for what they were—ellipses with the Sun at the focus—and each planet revolving in them with angular velocities which are inversely proportional to the instantaneous radius-vector. So long did it take to break the bondage of sterile Pythagorean tradition!

2 Decline and Renaissance

Following the peaks of achievements of the Hellenistic science, we have no real advances to report in the understanding of our place in the Universe around us for many centuries to come.

It is indeed remarkable to trace the way in which the genius of the human race is apt to erupt in spurts separated by long periods of slow gestation; and the age-long history of astronomy represents indeed no exception. The first steps to explore the structure of the inner precincts of the solar system were accomplished as a part of what is generally referred to as the 'Greek miracle', but not of the 'golden age of Greece'. During the time of Aischylos and Sophocles, Kallikrates or Feidias, Greek science was still relatively crude, and remained so through the sunset of the 'golden age' at the time of Pericles. It was not till after the effective breakdown of Athens and other Greek city-states as factors in contemporary power politics—after the breakdown of the short-lived empire of Alexander the Great, in fact—that the Greek (or, if you wish, Hellenistic, for other influences were many) scientific genius burst out in many directions, breaking previous bonds, and producing in a short time of efflorescence a magnificent pleiad of men like Aristarchos and Eratosthenes, or Archimedes and Apollonios— men who amply earned for Greece the attribute of the 'educator of mankind' and brought science to a level unsurpassed for at least 17 centuries—and beyond which it did not really advance until the time of the Renaissance. Seldom indeed, to use the common adage, so few did so much for so many!

The blessed period in the history of our subject, which produced the intellectual fruits reviewed in the preceding chapter, culminated in the 3rd century B.C. and lasted approximately one hundred years. Many theories have been advanced to account for this short duration. The Alexandrine adventure between 334–323 B.C. intermixed, and brought into sudden contact, more people of different races than ever before in a single decade—a fact which undoubtedly contributed to the intellectual ferment of the time. And what is perhaps more important, the disintegration of the Alexandrine empire following the death of the young conqueror in 323 B.C. produced a power vacuum in the Eastern Mediterranean and 'Magna Graecia', in which an almost uninterrupted peace prevailed, until the onslaught of the next world power, the Romans, on the Hellenistic world, which came a hundred years later.

It happened seldom indeed that so large a part of civilised humanity enjoyed peace for so long. This time, which also saw the emergence of a first cosmopolis—Alexandria—in which more than half a million inhabitants rubbed shoulders with each other, did not provide many examples of heroic or other extraordinary deeds to inspire artists to supreme creations. Men of science did not, however, need much terrestrial inspiration; they sought it in the sky and in the realm of geometry and numbers. As in the modern era in which we live, the ascendancy of science almost begins with a decline of the arts, and both can be brought to decay only by the brutal force of the barbarians.

The death of Archimedes in 212 B.C., during the sack of Syracuse, at the hand of a Roman soldier who found the scientist immersed in the midst of the battle in contemplation of his circles, has become almost symbolic in this connection; and the pilgrimage of Cicero to the tomb of Archimedes during his proconsulship in Sicily a century and a half later, reported by this prolific writer with snobbish satisfaction to his friends, smacks of the same hypocrisy to which we have since become accustomed in politicians. The stranglehold of ancient science was, to be sure, less dramatic or sudden than the death of Archimedes, but nonetheless effective. It was due to the Roman stolidity and indifference to everything that could not be put to practical use, which effectively extinguished the flame of free thought, as much as to its subsequent suppression by the Christians as well as the barbarians who overpowered the Mediterranean basin following the breakdown of the Roman Empire. By the time of Christian triumph and barbaric invasions, Graeco-Roman science was already but a pale ghost of its former old self, with much of it forgotten and lost beyond retrieval.

The transmission of continuity in modern science is ensured by so many agencies as to be almost automatic, and the individual scientist nowadays need not spend much effort to gain access to any source. On the other hand, in the ancient world—and even in the middle ages—the transmission of scientific information was a very uncertain process. If, in particular, one bears in mind the untold number of wars and other calamities that had occurred in the Mediterranean world since the days of Hellenistic civilisation, how did the writings of men like Aristarchos or Archimedes escape destruction, and in what form did they eventually reach us?

When Archimedes composed one of them—say the *Psammites* from which we quoted in the preceding chapter—the number of readers who could have been interested in it must have been severely limited from the outset, and have remained so throughout the centuries. It is unlikely that the 'first edition' issued by the author consisted of more than a dozen handwritten copies. Some of them may have found their way to the libraries of Alexandria or Pergamon; but those libraries were in time destroyed. Other copies may have been for a time preserved in private libraries, such as those of Archimedes himself, of the king Hieron or his son Gelon; but how much of a chance of survival did these possess? Did any one of them escape destruction at the sack of the Syracuse by the Romans in 212 B.C.? Did any palace of antiquity—anywhere in the world—come down to us with its contents intact? How did the books they once contained ever reach us, especially those which could never have enjoyed any degree of 'popularity'?

It is probable that the same questions must have also arisen in the minds of their authors, and that, as a result, men of science in bygone days did not always write up their discoveries as they would do today, because they may have thought 'What's the good of it? Whom will the text reach, and who will preserve it?' Inhibitions arising from such misgivings were probably a contributing cause to the slowness of progress in ancient times. Thus the relationship of Ptolemy to Hipparchos appears to us like that of a younger contemporary to his senior—and yet they were separated by almost three centuries in time! Moreover, the doubts which ancient authors must have had about the fate of their contributions to humanity were, unfortunately, only too often well-founded. Modern scholars agree that at least nine-tenths of all ancient scientific production never reached us in any form (except, perhaps, through cryptic allusions or references) and are totally lost, and how much of this lost knowledge concerned astronomy we shall never know.

The survival of the rest may indeed appear miraculous; and yet again it may not have been as rare an event as one might think. Ancient people had an almost superstitious respect for the written word, and esoteric writing in particular. This explains why the Greek MSS, even though of no use to the average person, were often jealously kept and transmitted from generation to generation—from owner to robber to looter, from looter to a new owner —until, from time to time, they fell into the hands of people who were sufficiently appreciative or enthusiastic to prepare new copies or translations, or add commentaries.

The Archimedean and other MSS which have finally reached us have thus very likely escaped not one catastrophe, but many. To be more specific, the oldest extant MS of the tract *On the Size and Distances of the Sun and the Moon* by Aristarchos survived as a part of the Codex Vaticanus Graecus 204, written sometime in the 10th century A.D. (a page of which is reproduced on the accompanying Figure 3—therefore, a thousand years before our time, but thirteen centuries after the composition of the original. Moreover, the oldest and most trustworthy extant MS of the *Psammites* of Archimedes, contained in Codex 28 of the Laurentian Library in Florence, hails only from the end of the 15th century, but appears to be a direct copy of another MS (now lost) going back to the 9th or 10th century of our era. The famous passage referring to Aristarchos' idea of the heliocentric system whose English translation (by T. L. Heath) we quoted on pp. 28–29, is reproduced in original on Figure 4 from the MS of the Laurentiana.

These are, therefore, our credentials for the historical veracity of the story outlined in the first chapter of this book. Both sources were, admittedly, written (or copied) at a time which is much closer to our age than to the time of their origin. What encourages us to hope that the text which reached us has not been corrupted by transmission in the course of some thirteen 'dark' centuries which separate the oldest extant copies from the originals? It is the fact that almost all medieval copyists and translators—whether Muslims, Jews or Christians—are known to have had one quality

Fig. 3. Facsimile of p. 110 (verso) of the Codex Vaticanus Graecus, No. 204, written some time in the 10th century A.D. which constitutes the oldest known copy of Aristarchos's tract *On the Size and Distances of the Sun and the Moon*. The page above contains a description of Aristarchos's method described on pp. 22–23 of this book. (By courtesy of Dr. D. J. K. O'Connell, S.J., Director of the Vatican Observatory)

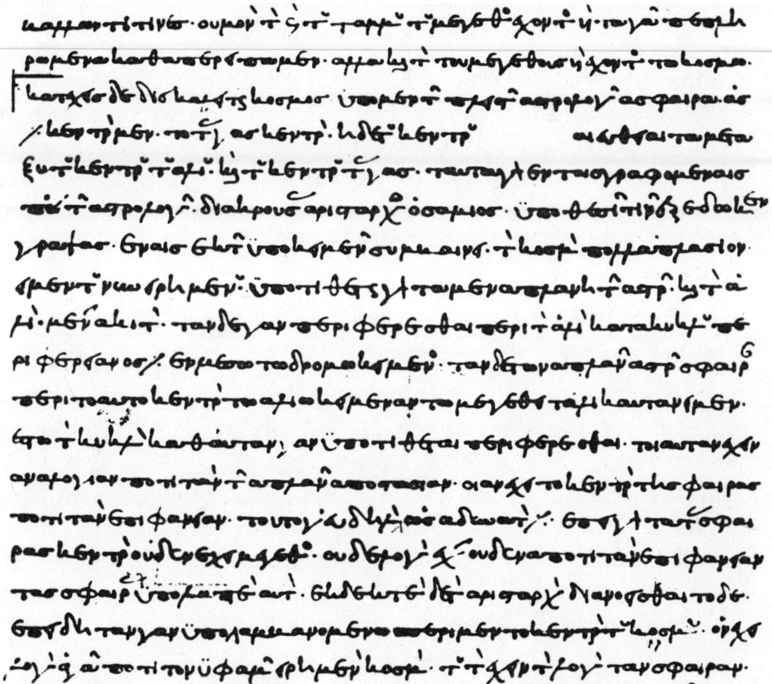

Fig. 4. A facsimile page of the oldest extant text of Archimedes's *Psammites* (Sand-Reckoner) from Codex 28 of the Laurentian Library in Florence, containing (between the marks) the famous passage on Aristarchos's ideas of the heliocentric planetary system, quoted in translation on pp. 28–29. The MS reproduced above goes back only to the 15th century; but represents a copy of a 9–10th-century MS which was still in existence around 1500 A.D. but has since disappeared.

39

in common: namely, they were invariably far more interested in the form than in the contents, and their reverence for the written word was such that their work was as a rule literal and pedantic. Therefore, such ancient MSS as were not destroyed by accident in the course of time could expect relatively faithful preservation because of the pedantic faithfulness of oral and written traditions.

FROM PTOLEMY TO COPERNICUS

'A dazzling light; a terrible storm; a deep darkness'—this is how the peak and decline of the Hellenistic civilization was recently summarized in a nutshell by a distinguished historian of mathematics. In actual fact, the situation was probably less dramatic or simple; and, in particular, the gradual downfall of astronomy from the heights of the hellenistic science to the darkness of the middle ages extended over several hundreds of years.

Not that the cultivation of astronomy ever ceased altogether, or that no significant personality has emerged after the commencement of our era. For Claudius Ptolemaeus—whose name remained almost synonymous with the science of astronomy for many centuries—was born in Egypt, and flourished in Alexandria in the second half of the 2nd century A.D. (died after 161 A.D.). His influence on later times in astronomy, mathematics and geography was second only to that of Aristotle—though (like with Aristotle) by virtue of his expository powers rather than originality of thought. His methods, as well as facts, were derived essentially from Hipparchos (in most cases, Ptolemy admitted this himself); yet it is largely through him—and, in particular, through his great treatise that became known mainly under its Arabic subtitle of *Almagest*—that Hipparchos' astronomy came down to us. Ptolemy was a man of the Euclidean type, and his approach, that of a mathematician. His chief contribution was his geometrical theory of planetary motions, involving the simultaneous use of eccentrics and epicycles, and his substitution of diagrams by mathematical expressions completed the establishment of astronomy as a mathematical discipline.

Ptolemy's entire system of cosmography constituted, however, no progress over the achievements of his hellenistic predecessors

—if anything, a step back. Ptolemy's solar system was strictly geocentric, and thus closed to any rational determination of its size. He vitiated even the knowledge of the dimensions of the Earth by his adoption of the wrong estimate of its size by Poseidonios (see p. 17), and, moreover, made the Sun only $5\frac{1}{2}$ times as large as the Earth.

Ptolemy was the last astronomer of antiquity of any note, and what followed him was a descent into an abyss of ignorance and superstition. As we peer at it through dim telescopes of historical research across a gulf of almost two millenia, we must not forget that the Graeco-Roman culture broke down under the stress of a terrible ordeal. Indeed, it perished only in the course of one of the greatest intellectual conflicts that ever rocked humanity, a clash between the old Greek ideals and the new Oriental religions, such as Christianity and Islam, and that gigantic struggle between lay and religious scales of values lasted for centuries. The Greeks laid stress upon truth and beauty; the Romans, upon strength and usefulness; while the Christians, upon charity and love.

The ultimate triumph of Christianity—at least in Europe—was a distinct gain from the moral point of view, but for scientific research it proved to be an unmitigated disaster. Unfortunately— as was once movingly expressed by Georges Sarton—most human beings are incapable of grasping an idea unless they exaggerate it to the exclusion of all others. In this case, most people who eventually understood that charity was essential did not stop there, but jumped to the conclusion that it was all-sufficient. This led them to consider scientific research to be not only useless, but pernicious. Thus the ruin of science, begun by Roman utilitarianism, came close to being completed by Christian piety. It has taken more than fifteen hundred years for the lesson to sink in that knowledge without charity, and charity without knowledge, are equally dangerous; and how many people have not understood it as yet!

To illustrate the rapid deterioration of the intellectual climate in the first few centuries of our era, listen to the following words by St. Augustine—one of the greatest Fathers of the Church— from his book *De Civitate Dei* written between 413–428 A.D. (i.e., less than three centuries after the time of Ptolemy).

'The good Christian should beware of mathematicians and of all those who make empty prophecies. The danger already exists that mathematicians have made a covenant with the devil to darken the spirit and confine man to the bonds of Hell.'

It is not charity, but ignorance which speaks to us through the pen of this saint of his church, and, unfortunately, the deeds of his co-religionists were sometimes far more damaging than words. Thus shortly before (around 400 A.D.) the famous Library of Alexandria—which underwent many vicissitudes in the course of its 700-year long existence—was finally destroyed by a Christian mob incited by Theophilos, Bishop of Alexandria, and with it the sources of much of the wisdom accumulated over centuries.

The story gained credence that the actual destruction did not take place until after 640 A.D., when the Muslims sacked Alexandria. The Khalif Umar is supposed to have said at that time: 'The text of those books is contained in the Koran or not. If it is, we do not need them; if it is not, they are pernicious'. This story may be (and probably is) apocryphal. However, there was not much, if anything, left of the original library to be destroyed at that time. The Christian fanatics must have argued in much the same way as their Muslim emulators. Moreover, the pagan books were far more dangerous to the Christians who could read them, than to the Muslims who could not read them at all.

This latter situation would, to be sure, not last for long. For as darkness descended on Western Europe, in the latter part of the first millenium of our era, the sun of civilisation rose over the Middle East, and much of the ancient literature survived through Arabic translations made at that time; while, in Europe, only priests and learned scribes, bent over the dwindling remnants of ancient texts, were dimly aware that humanity had known better times.

The nadir was reached in Europe some time around the 11th century of our time, and the early dawn of the budding renaissance appeared on the horizon in the 12th and 13th centuries. Like sleepers awakening from a long night, the inhabitants of Europe began to flex their intellectual muscles—first on rediscovering what had been lost during centuries of slumber, some of which had, in the meantime, been preserved through the intermediary of Arabic (or Hebrew) translations. It is impossible within the scope of this book to trace the vicissitudes through which the intellectual heritage of the ancients must have undergone during these 'dark centuries', but the oldest copies of the original Greek MSS which have been preserved (such as those by Aristarchos or Archimedes, referred to in the preceding chapter of this book) go back to those times, and from then the continuity of tradition remains essentially uninterrupted.

In picking up its threads in the 'autumn of the Middle Ages'—the age of Dante, Maimonides or Ibn Rushd—we should note one fact: namely, that while a good part of the astronomical knowledge of our Greek and Hellenistic ancestors survived in Arab translations, no contributions of any note have been added by the Arabs to the previous knowledge of cosmology. Many of the Arabic scholars who flourished between the 9th and 11th centuries—such as Al Battani (858–929 A.D.) or Al Zarquali (1029–1087 A.D.)—were astronomers of note, but their interests and contributions were mainly observational and descriptive; cosmological speculations occupied no greater part of their interests than had been the case with the Babylonian or Chaldean predecessors of the Greeks. In particular, questions relating to the structure of the solar system, or the dimensions of the Earth, seemed to hold no attraction for astronomers of the Near or Far East; and history shows that no real effort, let alone progress, in these respects had been made until the European thought began to emerge from the Middle Ages by the time of the Renaissance.

THE RENAISSANCE: Revival of the Heliocentric System

The term Renaissance in European history is usually employed to describe the awakening of arts and literature in the late Middle Ages; but as far as science itself was concerned, the thaw was long, and the spring slow to come. It is difficult indeed for us to imagine (or try to recapture) the state of mind of the solitary scholars of such an age—of any age that follows the long night after the breakdown of the civilisations which preceded them. One of the principal consequences has been a completely different attitude displayed towards the past and the future.

In fact, until a few centuries ago in the West, and until relatively recent times in the East, it was the past, and not the future, which dominated so largely men's minds. Modern man, who sets his life goals in what is to come, exhibits thereby an attitude of mind quite alien to that prevalent in most earlier days. Ancient Egypt, Greece, Rome, the vast Asiatic civilisations, even the Renaissance, did not look ahead for the ideals and inspirations of their existence, but sought them in their distant origins, in their ancient glories, their fabled heroes, or pristine virtues. Unlike the modern man who dreams of the world he will make or conquer, the pre-modern man's 'golden age' was always in the past, not in the future! And if we use this criterion to divide modern times from the ancient as far as their division reflects itself in the science of astronomy, the actual watershed would not be encountered until some time in the 17th century—i.e., during a period which will occupy us in the next chapter of this book.

In the preceding chapter we have already emphasized that the 'golden age' of Greece (5th–4th century B.C.) earned its proud title by the superiority of its achievements in art and literature, though, in the field of science, it could not compare with the accomplishments of the subsequent 'hellenistic age' when, politically as well as artistically, Greece was already in decline. The same situation we shall now meet in the Renaissance, when the efflorescence of arts and literature—the time of Dante, Leonardo or Michelangelo—preceded the age of Galileo and Kepler by several generations. The life of Michelangelo spanned almost a whole century, and Galileo Galilei—the senior of the two 'founding fathers' of modern astronomy—was not born until the year of his death.

It is but a slight error—if error it be at all—to picture the life horizons of most scholars in the 14th and 15th centuries as essentially unchanged from what they had been in the hellenistic age and the early centuries of our era. It was not until the course of the 14th century that the process of rediscovery of the ancient scientific knowledge was well-nigh completed; and during the 15th century the first actual advances beyond the achievements of the ancients had been made through the work of such outstanding Central Europeans as Georg Peurbach (1423–1461) or Johann Müller (1436–1476) better known under his latinized name of Regiomontanus.

As far as cosmography was concerned, however, the Renaissance proved to be an age of disorder and compromises until its very end. At the beginning of the Renaissance, Ptolemy's *Alma-*

gest with its picture of the world was still the standard treatise on astronomy (as it had been for more than a thousand years before), and, since the invention of printing, could be read in Latin translations (published in 1515 and 1528) or in the Greek original since the appearance of its editio princeps in 1538. Shortly thereafter, the heliocentric model of the solar system was elaborated by Copernicus in his famous treatise *De Revolutionibus Orbium Celestium* (Nürnberg, 1543), reviving Greek traditions which had been thrown into darkness by Ptolemy's expository talents—and to this revival we wish now to turn our attention.

Nicolaus Copernicus—the greatest personality of Renaissance astronomy—led a life that is not too rich in biographical facts. Born in 1473 at Torun from a family of Polish burghers, he received his first university training in Kraków between 1491–1494; and under the patronage of his uncle, Bishop Lucas Watzelrode, he proceeded then to Italy where between 1496–1506 he spent the best years of his life at the Universities of Bologna, Padua and Ferrara, in preparation for an ecclesiastical career. When it was no longer possible for him to extend his leave from his homeland, he returned to Poland in 1506 to take up an office in the church which led to a canonry at the Frauenberg Cathedral in Warmia; and there, in the northern mists not far from the Baltic shores—a land so different from the sunny Italy of his youth—he was destined to spend the rest of his life.

Copernicus's interest in astronomy was awakened at Krakow University by his first outstanding teacher, Jan Brudzewski; but blossomed out in the finest flower which the Renaissance contributed to astronomy during his Italian years. Little is known of his life abroad, or of the influences to which he was exposed in Bologna and Padua (where Mario Novara must have been one of his masters). There is, however, no doubt that during his fifteen years of University life—at home and abroad—he learned all that ancient sources had to offer at that time. It is, moreover, more than probable that, on his return to Poland in 1506, he brought back with him at least the germ of the idea whose execution was to occupy him for the remaining thirty-seven years of his life, and to immortalize his name in the annals of our science: namely, a synthesis of the heliocentric system of Aristarchos with the geometrical apparatus of Ptolemaic astronomy.

That Copernicus learned in Italy of Aristarchos and his idea of the heliocentric system is established beyond any doubt, for Copernicus referred to Aristarchos in the MS (still extant) of his own book *De Revolutionibus*, although the respective passage was left out of the printed edition of his work by a stroke of the author's pen (see Figure 5). And, of course, Ptolemaic astronomy constituted the 'celestial mechanics' of the day with which each student of the subject had to become familiar.

Copernicus doubtless knew from his teachers (and, partly, from his own observations) that the heliocentric system, pure and simple, cannot be made to represent the apparent motions of the planets in the sky within the limits of accuracy of the observations even in the pre-telescopic era. This is why Hipparchos with Ptolemy introduced their complicated systems of epicycles. In order to 'save the phenomena', Copernicus felt constrained to adopt the same makeshift, but in place of doing so with the geocentric orbits of the celestial bodies, he set out to graft it onto a heliocentric system. He was the first to attempt such a synthesis, and his stature in the history of science rests on this fact.

Respect for truth compels us to admit that such a synthesis did not accomplish very much, nor could it; for Copernicus was still fully under the spell of the fateful Pythagorean dogma that motions of celestial bodies must be circular and uniform. It was these misconceptions, rather than the relative position of the Sun, which were primarily responsible for the protracted failure of astronomers to represent the apparent motions of the planets with sufficient accuracy, and a release from its evil charm was still a hundred years in the future by the time when Copernicus was returning from Italy to his homeland.

There are indications that Copernicus himself was aware of the difficulty (if not the futility) of his task; and the labour pains of the birth of his system extended over all his life. What is more, the older he grew, the more secretive he became about it. Gradually, however, the news leaked out even from his faraway corner of the world of the task undertaken by the ageing canon, and largely through the help of Georg Joachim von Lauchen (better known under the Latinised name of Rhaeticus)—who became his *fidus Achates* and played a role in this connection not dissimilar to that in which Edmond Halley was to coax out of the unwilling Isaac

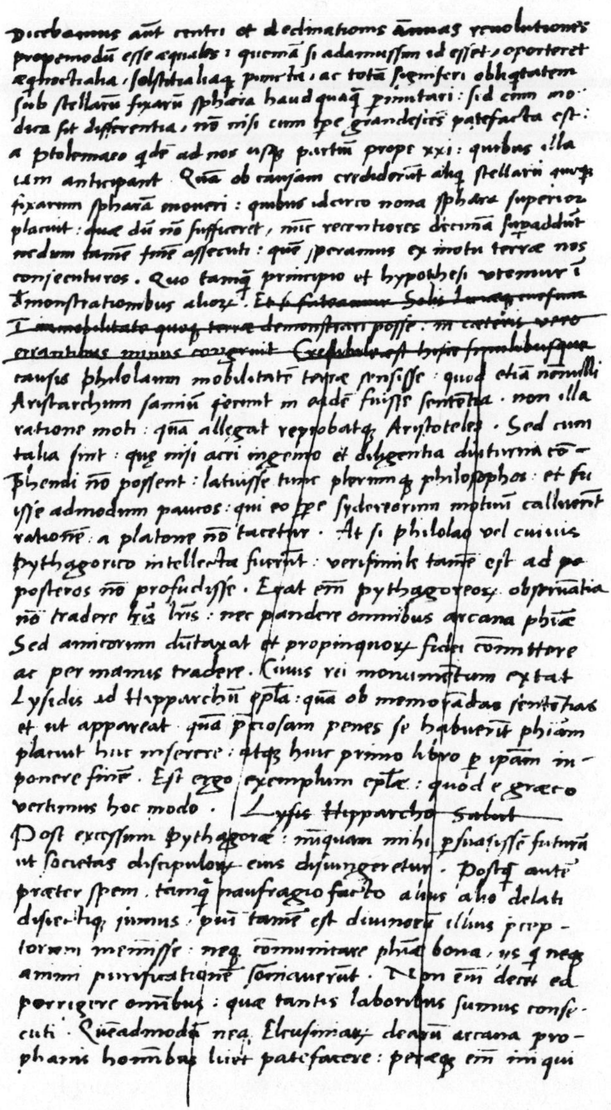

Fig. 5. A facsimile page of the manuscript of Copernicus's book, *De Revolutionibus Orbium Celestium* (Nürnberg, 1543), on which a reference to Aristarchos of Samos was crossed out by the author before the text was printed. (By courtesy of the Warsaw University Library).

Newton his *Principia* a century and a half later—Copernicus' *magnum opus*, containing the gist of his work and entitled *De Revolutionibus Orbium Celestium*, was to see the light of day at Nürnberg in 1543. Tradition has it that Copernicus received its first copy on his deathbed.

'Copernicus mortuus—nata scientia'; how much truth is there in this tradition which subsequent centuries have spun around the astronomer and his work? Very little. First, Copernicus did not invent the heliocentric model of the solar system, but consciously revived its ancient tradition going back to pre-Ptolemaic days. His personal contribution was to combine the heliocentric system with Ptolemaic geometry—kinematically still under the Pythagorean lore—but Copernicus was the first to develop this idea into a comprehensive system. He was, therefore, not a boldly original thinker, but a crystallizer of thought—much the same as could be said of Ptolemy fifteen centuries before.

To what extent does the work actually accomplished by Copernicus correspond to the tradition which has developed around it? In an attempt to answer this question, let us first recall that—contrary to most popular conceptions—the centre of the Copernican model of the solar system was not the Sun, but the geometrical centre of the circular orbit of the Earth, revolving around nothing in particular; for the position of the Sun was placed by him some distance of this centre. Moreover, in order to reconcile his geometrical models with the observations (mostly ancient; for Copernicus made very few of his own) within 10 minutes of arc—this was the extent of Copernicus' efforts—it was necessary to let the planets revolve along more epicycles ('wheels upon wheels') than required by the alternative geocentric system. The latter, in the hands of Georg Peurbach (in his *Epistomae*) required only 40 epicycles to 'save the phenomena', while the final system of Copernicus required 48 of them, i.e., eight more than the contemporary geocentric one! It is true that the heliocentric system relieved the outer planets of their principal epicycles representing their retrograde motion (which were simply resolved as a reflex of the motion of the terrestrial observer), but others were needed in their stead, and the over-all picture of the Ptolemaic system (see Figure 6) of the 16th century was essentially no more complicated geometrically than that of Copernicus (Figure 7).

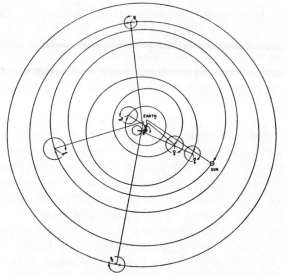

Fig. 6. A Ptolemaic Model of the Solar System (according to W. D. Stahlman; reproduced by courtesy of Dr. G. de Santillana).

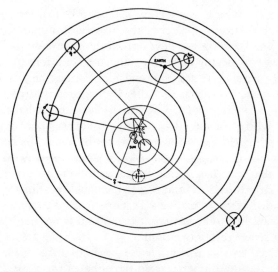

Fig. 7. The Copernican (1543) Model of the Solar System (according to W. D. Stahlman; reproduced by courtesy of Dr. G. de Santillana).

What is more important for the main topic of this book, the work of Copernicus did not represent any significant advance in our knowledge of the true size of the solar system. For Ptolemy in the 2nd century A.D. the distance to the Sun was 610 Earth diameters (the true value being 11 500) a value which Copernicus diminished to 571. In the geocentric system, the ratios of planetary distances are essentially arbitrary. Some idea of their proportions could, to be sure, be obtained from the light variations exhibited by the planetary motion, but the discovery of a law governing the variation of the intensity of a light source with the distance was still far in the future, and even the fact that the apparent diameter of the Moon failed to vary in accordance with the motions prescribed to it by Ptolemy was not taken as proof of their unreality. On the other hand, the heliocentric model contains a built-in system for determination of the relative size of planetary orbits in terms of that of the Earth (the annual 'retrograde' motion of each outer planet being merely a reflex of our own motion around the Sun). To this extent, Copernicus was the first to unravel for us at least the essential features of the model; but he underestimated its scale some twenty times.

Such were, in brief, the accomplishments of Copernicus, and the basis of his claims for a place in the history of our subject. Did he, in particular, develop any new astronomy? Scarcely so, for Copernicus was too deeply rooted in ancient traditions to make any conscious attempt at any original innovation; and as far as the main obstacle to progress—the Pythagorean lore of circular motions—was concerned, Copernicus was an unshakeable traditionalist who proclaimed his faith on several occasions with a zealotry which leaves no room for doubt about his convictions. Thus, in his *Letter against Werner*, written in 1524, Copernicus declared that '. . . It is fitting for us to follow the methods of the ancients strictly and to hold fast to their observations which have been handed down to us like a Testament. And to him who thinks that they are not to be entirely trusted in this respect, the gates of our Science are certainly closed'.

And listen to his earlier *Commentariolus* of 1514: 'Our ancestors assumed a large number of celestial spheres for a special reason: to explain the apparent motion of the planets by the principle of regularity. For they thought it altogether absurd that a heavenly

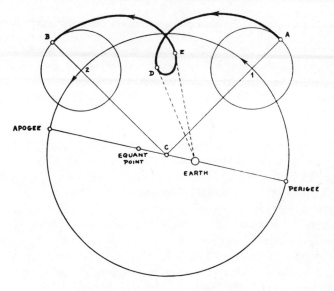

Fig. 8. Geometry of the Epicycles.

body should not always move with uniform velocity in a perfect circle'. And, as these Pythagorean tenets failed to 'save the phenomena' to the desired accuracy, Copernicus went on, 'Having become aware of these defects, I often considered whether there could perhaps be found a more reasonable arrangement of circles . . . in which everything would move uniformly about its proper centre, as the rule of absolute motion requires'.

And in this respect it may be fairly said that Copernicus outdid Ptolemy in his rigid adherence to the Pythagorean lore. For— from the strictly Pythagorean point of view—the Ptolemaic system was logically defective in one respect: namely, in placing the terrestrial observer, not at the geometrical centre of the planetary circular orbits, but a little off-centre (at what Ptolemy called the 'punctum equans'), in a position from which planetary motions could be made to appear to us to be uniform. This geometrical makeshift offended Copernicus's reverence for Pythagorean dogmas, and in his patient plodding way he set out to reject it by abolishing the 'equants' from his geometry—but only at the price of introducing more 'deferents' (i.e., auxiliary circles rolling like 'wheels on wheels' of the main circular orbits), and thus making the planetary clockwork more complicated.

Four hundred years before the time of Copernicus, the great Arab philosopher Ibn Rushd (1126–1198) already remarked that ... 'Ptolemaic astronomy is nothing in so far as existence is concerned; but it is convenient for computations of the non-existent'. Copernicus, who grafted this sterile offshoot on to a sounder and more ancient line of thought, would hardly have appreciated that kind of a joke, and throughout his life he carried on with his hopeless task with dreary seriousness. He has no real claim to be regarded as an actual forerunner of men like Galileo or Kepler who, a century later, were to call themselves Copernicans, and whose bold departures from tradition would have horrified their master's conservative soul. No, Copernicus was not one of them. He was, instead, the last of the great ancients—a spiritual companion of Hipparchos or Ptolemy. This is his rightful place in the history of science, a place in which he was soon to find himself on the other side of the 'great divide' after 1610; but by the time of Copernicus's death this was still 67 years in the future.

How was the Copernican synthesis of the system of Aristarchos dressed up in the garb of Ptolemaic geometry, received in the meantime by the contemporaries of Copernicus and by his immediate descendents? It was accepted with lukewarm interest on the part of the educated Catholic clergy, and without demur by Pope Paul III to whom Copernicus's book was dedicated. The Lutheran church, on the other hand, objected to it strongly from the outset on grounds of biblical fundamentalism. Martin Luther himself gave out a few uncouth growls ('That fool wants to turn the whole art of astronomy upside down') in his native vernacular, while Melanchthon proved the Earth to be at rest in elegant Latin. Theological controversies have eventually become so rancorous that both Protestants and Catholics, for propaganda purposes, began to outbid each other in their denunciation of the heliocentric system. But the full fury of it did not come till a hundred years later.

And the astronomers? They became increasingly exasperated by this schism of cosmological double-think, aggravated by gradually accumulating and more accurate observations which neither doctrine—Ptolemaic or Copernican—could satisfactorily account for. Nothing personified the existing messiness better than the life and accomplishments of Tycho Brahe, which we wish to recall here.

THE FORERUNNER: Tycho Brahe

Tycho Brahe, a veritable 'prince of astronomers', (called so not only because of his noble origin, but for more valid reasons), dominated by his work and personality the astronomy of the second half of the 16th century, and his career brought the astronomy of the ancients to its climax as well as its virtual close. In fact, his observational achievements were destined to make him the veritable John the Baptist of modern astronomy; and, although modesty was not one of his main virtues, he remained unaware of it till the end of his life.

Born in 1546 of a family of grandseigneurs of the Hamlet country, and distinguished by military rather than scientific exploits, Tycho turned his attention to astronomy during the early years of his university life. The principal cause of his conversion to a calling, then regarded still as unbecoming for a nobleman, was the apparition of a 'new star'—the famous supernova in the constellation of Cassiopeia in 1572. This event was not unique in the history of astronomy (a similar phenomenon in the year 1054 passed almost without notice in Europe), but proved so spectacular that Tycho virtually never turned his eyes from the sky ever after, until the time of his death. With the support of King Frederick II of Denmark, he set up on the island of Hveen an observatory—named by Tycho symbolically the Uraniborg—a place which for a time resumed in the world the role of the famous 15th century observatory of Ulugh Bek in Samarkand. There, for more than twenty years (between 1576–1597) Tycho lorded over his entourage and flock, making his own instruments, carrying out the observations, and printing his own publications.

His haughty disposition and overbearing acts, carried to their limits, eventually brought about Tycho's downfall and exile from his homeland. In 1597, he had to leave Hveen (with some of his instruments, to be sure) to wander for many months through Europe like a comet with his retinue, until, in 1599, he found a haven in Prague, capital of the Kingdom of Bohemia, at the court of the Emperor Rudolph II. Unfortunately, not many years of peace were vouchsafed to him on Bohemian soil, for he died there in 1601—barely 55 years old—but not before he performed his last great service to astronomy: to invite to Prague Johannes Kepler as his collaborator. For, in doing so, Tycho directly precipitated events which soon thereafter brought about the final downfall of the Pythagorean lore with all the astronomy of the ancients, and enthroned the heliocentric solar system in its true form.

What were the principal contributions of Tycho Brahe to astronomy before that time? By all his talents and inclinations he was predominantly an observer, and one of the greatest of all time —a fitting link in the long historical chain extending from Hipparchos through Tycho to Bradley and Bessel of more modern times. For it is precisely an observer that was needed at this stage to precipitate crystallization of cosmological thought, and Tycho performed his historical task in a grand manner. His instruments— sextants and armillae—were still essentially the tools of the ancients, and differed in principle but little from those used by Regiomontanus more than a hundred years before. But by meticulous attention to craftsmanship, and the care with which he calibrated them or investigated their errors, Tycho set the ultimate limit to a precision with which one could measure the positions of celestial bodies in the sky during the pre-telescopic era.

Modern discussions of his observations disclose that Tycho's positions (duly freed from refraction) were accurate to within less than one minute of arc (i.e., one-thirtieth of the apparent diameter of the Sun or the Moon)—or ten times as accurate as those at the disposal of Copernicus half a century before. In fact, Tycho's skill as an observer—unrivalled as it remained until the time of Bradley in the early part of the 18th century—so impressed his contemporaries as well as immediate successors that astronomers adhered to his naked-eye methods for positional measurements until more than fifty years after the discovery of the telescope!

The primary observational goal which Tycho set for himself and his school was an accurate re-determination of the lunar and planetary motions: in particular, of that of Mars. The epoch-making nature of this contribution will not transpire until the next chapter, in connection with their interpretation by Johannes Kepler. It was these data which enabled Kepler at last to chase out of astro-

Fig. 9. **TYCHO BRAHE**
(1546–1601)

"Nec fasces, nec opes, sola artis sceptra perennant".

nomy the two-thousand year old ghost of Pythagorean misconceptions. But other, more immediate achievements of Tycho, also helped to bring down the ancient edifice of Aristotelian cosmology. His proof of the absence of any measurable proper motion of the 'new star' of 1562—thus relegating this object in the 'eighth sphere' of fixed stars—helped to demolish the ancient notion of the immutability of the heavens. Or his observations disclosing no measurable parallax for the comets of 1577 and 1585 placed the latter not less than seven times as far from us as the Moon—thereby destroying the Aristotelian notion that comets were 'sub-lunar' phenomena. One corner after another of the outmoded edifice was inexorably crumbling down under the blows administered to it by Tycho's observational zeal. But one of the old props still held: namely, the absence of an annual parallax of fixed stars.

As had been realised already by Aristarchos in the 3rd century B.C., a heliocentric model of the solar system in which our Earth revolves around the Sun with all the rest of the planets would require all distant light sources—such as the stars—to exhibit an apparent annual motion in the sky, representing a reflex of the actual motion of the Earth. This apparent parallactic motion should be circular in a direction perpendicular to the plane of the Earth's orbit (i.e., at the 'pole of the ecliptic'), and elliptical in any direction inclined to it, the size of the ellipse representing, in effect, the size of the terrestrial orbit around the Sun viewed from the distance of the object in question. This is a necessary consequence of the heliocentric model (revolving Earth); on the geocentric one (stationary Earth) no parallax would be expected, and the positions of the stars on the (rotating) celestial sphere could remain truly fixed.

What was the verdict of the observations on the existence of such parallactic motions in Tycho's days? There is no room for doubt that it was this problem—the parallax of the fixed stars, or rather the absence of it—which exercised Tycho's skill to the utmost and worried him deeply, for he was fully aware of its crucial significance. His angular measurements, he knew, were accurate enough to detect the annual parallax of a star amounting to no more than one minute of arc—and yet none was apparent! Did this mean that the radius of the sphere of fixed stars (all stars were still thought to be at essentially the same distance from us) could be more than 3000 times farther away from the Sun than the Earth? The audacity of such a conception did not deter Aristarchos (as we know from the testimony of Archimedes, printed on p. 29) in the 3rd century B.C.; but was too much for Tycho, and constituted one of the principal reasons why this prince of astronomers of his age refused to accept the heliocentric system.

He had, to be sure, other reasons as well; and equally important to him was the fact that the heliocentric astronomy (even in the Copernican garb) failed to represent the motions of the planets in the sky within the limits of his observational errors—far from it! In other words, Tycho Brahe repudiated the Copernican system for similar reasons as may have led Hipparchos of old to reject the geometrically simpler heliocentric system of Aristarchos: it simply did not 'save the phenomena' in a satisfactory manner. Besides, outstanding as Tycho was as the observer and instrumentalist, his physical intuition was clearly weak and unimaginative ('how could the fat and lazy Earth be capable of motions ascribed to it by Copernicus?' he lamented on one occasion).

In place of the heliocentric system which he thus rejected, Tycho set out to resurrect an even older tradition of Heracleides, in accordance with which all planets are actually satellites of the Sun, this 'solar system' as well as the Moon revolves actually around the Earth as the centre of the Universe. Whether or not a system so constructed could represent the observed motions of the planets any better than that of Copernicus, Tycho did not know nor could he prove it, for he was no mathematician, and on his deathbed he implored Johannes Kepler to do so in his stead.

But Kepler—that anima candida in a tumultuous age—was willing enough to defend his master in his polemics against Ursus or in other lesser affairs, but not in his cosmology. When Tycho's body was being laid to rest on the 4th day of November, 1601, in the Týn Church of Prague amidst all the pomp and splendour due to the departed Imperial Mathematician, he was leaving behind him a legacy that already contained the verdict which—as we shall see—would have satisfied none of the parties that contended so far for the explanation of the kinematics of the solar system, but took a turn unexpected to all.

Which way the verdict went will be explained in the next chapter. In paying, in this place, homage to Tycho we must admit that, like Copernicus, Tycho was not a creative genius or a founder of new cosmology, but a giant of methodical observation; and this is what was needed at his time above everything else. There were enough theories in the field already, all with their roots in ancient traditions, and it was clearly up to the observations to single out the correct one. This was, in fact, done—though not by Tycho himself, but by Kepler on the basis of Tycho's observations of the planet Mars; and the day was veritably around the corner when, after two millenia of gradual groping, at least the kinematics of the solar system would be settled for ever (though for the establishment of its true scale we shall have to wait almost another century). But to explain how this came to pass will be the object of the next chapter.

3 New Astronomy

THE FOUNDING FATHERS

Astronomy is one of the oldest sciences conceived by the human mind, and a retrospective look at its age-long story reveals its course to run like a meandering river, with long quiescent periods of slow gestation interrupted now and then by rapids—when new vistas suddenly opened up to widen unexpectedly our horizons. One such period occurred in the 3rd century B.C., when in a span of less than a hundred years Aristarchos, Eratosthenes, Archimedes and Apollonios—to name only the greatest—injected enough intellectual ferment to sustain our science with inspiration for centuries to come. By the time of the Renaissance, however, the most part of the momentum provided by antiquity had already been spent, and improving observational techniques were exposing discrepancies between theory and observations, which clamoured for a new approach. Matters came, indeed, to a climax in the first decade of the 17th century, when the ship of our science found itself engulfed in rapids, in which much of the dead ballast carried over from preceding ages was finally thrown overboard, and a course set which led directly to the modern astronomy as we know it today.

As often happens in the annals of science, when the situation becomes ripe for major developments, these may be precipitated by more than one independent event; and so it was in our present case. Chance willed it, moreover, that the two independent—and quite unrelated—events to which modern astronomy owes its birth can be dated to the same year of 1609. That year—one of the most memorable ones in the long history of our subject—Johannes Kepler published his *Astronomia Nova* with the discovery of the two of his famous laws of planetary motion which, with one stroke placed celestial mechanics on a firm footing; and, within but months of this milestone, Galileo Galilei introduced the telescope into astronomical use, which led to the untold widening of our horizons in space. The impact of both these initially unrelated events was soon to transform astronomy from the capricious trickle of a brook into the mighty stream it was later to become; and the personalities towering over this juncture like Founding Fathers, were Johannes Kepler with Galileo Galilei, to be joined by the end of the same century by Isaac Newton.

As the life and work of the principals are inseparably connected in this dramatic episode in the history of our science, in what follows we shall outline the full significance of their respective achievements on the background of some biographical data. For only in this way can we attempt to recapture the spirit and excitement of those truly breathtaking times. And, for the sake of continuity, we propose to commence with Kepler—the younger of the two Founding Fathers—because his work was so intimately connected with that of the preceding generation, while Galileo happened to initiate an entirely unexpected path.

JOHANNES KEPLER: Beginning of Celestial Mechanics

Johannes Kepler, a German astronomer, whose personality and work tower in the history of the physical sciences between those of Copernicus and Newton symbolising a transition from ancient traditions to modern times, was born on December 27th, 1571, in Weil (at that time a Free City in the Holy Roman Empire, and later of the Kingdom of Würtemberg) as a scion of a declining old family of minor gentry. His frail health predestined him early to the career of a scholar. After leaving the Convent School of Adelberg monastery, he was admitted to the Swabian University of Tübingen in 1589, where he spent three years studying theology, mathematics and philosophy. Astronomy seems to have played at first a subordinate role in Kepler's education, though it was already at Tübingen that he received from Michael Mästlin an introduction to Copernican astronomy, the defence and propagation of which became one of the great tasks of his life.

On completion of his studies, Kepler intended to dedicate himself to the service of the (Protestant) Church; but his independence of spirit and lack of orthodoxy led his masters to recommend him,

Fig. 10.　　　　　**JOHANNES KEPLER**
(1571–1630)
Discoverer of the Model of the Solar System.

instead, for a professorship in mathematics in the protestant Academy in Graz (Upper Styria). This became Kepler's first professional position and deflected his career to astronomy.

His first work, a juvenile booklet entitled *Prodromus . . . sive Mysterium Cosmographicum* (Tübingen 1596), shows its author reaching for the law of 'quantization' of planetary orbits, an effort which proved to be altogether on the wrong track. The originality and boldness of its subject revealed, however, such talent as to attract to its 25-year-old author the attention of the contemporary prince of astronomers, Tycho de Brahe, who shortly invited Kepler to join him at the Benátky Castle, near Prague, as a collaborator in his efforts to interpret theoretically the observed positions of the planets accumulated by Tycho during his lifetime.

Kepler answered the call (prompted as he was also by the religious difficulties at Graz), and joined Tycho at Prague from January 1600. This memorable conjunction of the two leading astronomers of their time—the ageing great observer destined to hand over his observational treasures to the brilliant young theoretician—lasted only through twenty-two stormy months and ended abruptly through Tycho's premature death on October 24th of 1601. Kepler was, however, then climbing rapidly to the zenith of his career. Such was the impression he created in so short a time at Prague that, only a few days after Tycho's death, Rudolph II (a shadowy monarch who dedicated his life to fostering arts and sciences rather than power politics) named Kepler his Imperial Mathematician (in succession to Tycho)—a position which Kepler held, actually or by name, for the rest of his life.

The ensuing decade at Prague (1602–1612) proved to be the high noon of the life of the new Imperial Mathematician and a memorable time in the history of astronomical science. For it was then that the time came to pass for the new astronomy to see the light of day; and it was Tycho's observations of the planet Mars which, in Kepler's hands, eventually furnished the clue. The last stage of this centuries-long effort was indeed well set, for, by a fortunate accident, the problem of Mars' motion came up for Tycho's attention at the time when Kepler came to join him in Bohemia. 'I believe it was an act of Divine Providence' Kepler commented later on, 'that I arrived just at the time when Longomontanus [another one of Tycho's assistants] was occupied with Mars. For

Mars alone enables us to penetrate the secrets of astronomy which otherwise would remain forever hidden from us'. The reason is, of course, the fact that (as we now know, and Kepler soon learned!) the orbit of Mars exhibits a relatively large eccentricity ($e=0.093$), which makes the deficiencies of the ancient cult of the circles particularly glaring. No other planet would have led Kepler so securely to his goal!

At the beginning, of course, Mars meant nothing but trouble. Kepler set out first to determine from Tycho's data the position of the Martian line of apsides (i.e., the direction of a line connecting the points at which Mars is closest and furthest from the Sun) and of the place on it for the Sun and the Earth—a problem which could not be solved by any direct method known at that time. In the absence of such methods, Kepler attempted to do so by trial and error. 'If this cumbersome mode of work displeases you' he addressed the readers of Chapter 18 of his *Astronomia Nova*, 'you may rightly pity me, who had to apply it at least seventy times with great loss of time; so you will not wonder that the fifth year is already passing since I began with Mars . . . Acute geometers equal to Vieta may show that my method is not at the state of the art . . . May they solve the problem in their way. For me it suffices that . . . to find the way out of this labyrinth I had, instead of the torch of geometry, an artless thread guiding me to the exit'. Kepler was indeed no geometer of the calibre of Copernicus or Newton. He preferred numerical computations, then only just beginning to be aided by the use of logarithms. But even as a computer Kepler was no prodigy, for some 900 pages of his worksheets—still extant—show evidence of many slips which had to be corrected at later stages, and some never were!

The results of his computations in the first part of his work succeeded in reproducing the positions of the Martian perihelia, as well as aphelia, observed between 1580–1604, with errors well within $1\frac{1}{2}$ minutes of arc. As this was also about the precision of Tycho's observations, Kepler's task would seem to have been completed. Chapter 18 of his book closed on this optimistic tone, only for the next chapter to begin with the words: 'Whoever would think it possible? This hypothesis . . . so well in accordance with the oppositions, is nevertheless wrong!' This became apparent as soon as Kepler used the same elements to compute the real distances of the planet from observed latitudes. The differences between theory and observations at the times of quadratures turned out to amount to almost 8 minutes of arc! Such discrepancies were encountered before, by Ptolemy (or, for that matter, by Copernicus); but they did not worry them unduly, because their observations were not that good.

But this attitude was no longer permissible after 1600 A.D., for, as Kepler noted, 'It behoves us, to whom by divine benevolence such a very careful observer as Tycho Brahe had been given, in whose observations an error of 8 minutes (of arc) of Ptolemy's computation could be disclosed, to recognise this boon of God with thankful mind, and use it by exerting ourselves in working out the true form of celestial motions . . . Thus these single eight minutes indicate to us the road towards the renovation of the entire astronomy; they afforded the material for a large part of this work'.

The battle of the young David with the Goliath of the 'epistemological trash' of the ancients was now joined in earnest, and fifty subsequent chapters of the *Astronomia Nova* bear witness to this epic struggle. Again and again Kepler charged, from a different direction, at the heart of his problem. By the time he reached the 14th chapter, the Pythagorean axiom of uniform motion had already gone overboard. In what followed Kepler began to feel that even the more exalted one of the circular motions may have to follow; but not until (in Chapters 41–44) he tried for the last time, with almost savage thoroughness, to attribute a circular orbit to Mars and failed; thus ending Chapter 44 with the confession that . . . 'The conclusion is quite simply that the planet's path is not a circle; it curves inward on both sides and outward again at the opposite ends. Such a curve is called an oval. The orbit of Mars is, therefore, not a circle, but an oval figure'.

But what kind of an oval? The reader of Kepler's book can follow in the next six chapters the master's anguished beating about the bush, without seeing for long the obvious. Still, by the end of 1604, Kepler wrote to his friend Fabricius 'how simple it would be if the orbit of Mars were a perfect ellipse'—as though the possibility that the orbit is indeed an ellipse has not entered his mind. The ultimate realisation that this was the case came apparently quite suddenly; and 'When I realised this . . .', Kepler wrote,

'I felt as it I had been awakened from a sleep . . . Ah, what a foolish bird I have been.'

We can almost hear the sigh of relief when the torment was over. The rest of his work was a mopping-up operation, and a removal of the scaffold from the edifice which contained, as the corner-stones of modern astronomy, the formulation of Kepler's first two immortal laws, disclosing that:

1. each planet revolves around the Sun in an ellipse, with the Sun situated at its focus; and,
2. the angular velocity of each planet in its orbit varies in inverse proportion to the square of the instantaneous radius-vector.

Actually, the 'second law' was discovered first, and in arriving at it Kepler resorted to a process anticipating in fact some operations of infinitesimal calculus—a process having its roots in the 'method of exhaustion' conceived by Archimedes two thousand years before, and which, before the end of the century—through the work of Newton—will justify Kepler's laws as integrals of motion of two bodies in an inverse-square force field.

Kepler's work described above was completed during his first years in Prague, under the constant pressure of financial and family worries, of delicate health, of difficulties with Tycho's heirs as to the disposal of the observations, and of many other matters. By the end of 1604 his results were essentially complete, and in 1605 he could present the manuscript to the Emperor.

The Emperor's command to have it printed at his own expense was, alas, easier said than done, for the imperial treasury in Rudolph's day suffered from chronic lack of money, so that it was not until the summer of 1609 that the printed book finally saw the light of day in Heidelberg, under the proud title of *Astronomia Nova, aitiologetos seu Physica Coelestis* (New Astronomy, causally explained; or Celestial Physics), preceding the sub-title *De Motu Stellae Martis* Ex Observationibus Tychonis Brahe . . . Plurium annorum pertinaci studio elaborata Pragae (on the Motion of the Star Mars, elaborated from Tycho Brahe's observations in Prague after several years of assiduous work)—an arrangement by which Kepler emphasized the fact that, in its contents, Mars served only as a tool to wider aims.

The publication of this book marks (together with the almost simultaneous discovery of the telescope) truly the beginnings of modern astronomy, and its importance cannot be over-estimated. Together with Ptolemy's *Almagest*, Copernicus's *De Revolutionibus* and Newton's *Principia*, it constitutes one of the cornerstones of modern science. It was Kepler—not Copernicus—who thus placed the Sun at the centre of the solar system, and described planetary orbits by a simple model of far-reaching exactitude— sufficient to account in its simplicity not only for the naked-eye observations of Tycho Brahe, but also for the telescopic observations of decades to come. Such small deviations as were discovered later are fully understood in terms of Newtonian mechanics as caused by mutual planetary perturbations. Gone, and relegated to their proper historical place, were all the Pythagorean misconceptions, with all the epicycles of Hipparchos or Ptolemy which hung like a millstone around the neck of astronomy until the end of the Renaissance. Well did Kepler himself qualify (in a letter to Longomontanus) his own achievement as the 'cleansing of the Augean stables'.

But he did much more. Unlike Copernicus and the ancients, Kepler was concerned not only with a geometrical description of planetary motions, but also with their causes, and this he emphasized by the words 'Celestial Physics, causally explained'. Although this latter aspect of his work exceeds by far the scope of our present book, suffice it to say that Kepler was clearly aware that the motive power of planetary motions rested in the Sun, and that the force of this power falls off with increasing distance—thus intuitively anticipating gravity. In Kepler's later writings (*The Somnium*), moreover, the idea flickered once or twice that this force falls off with the inverse square of the distance. This was, of course, only a surmise which Kepler was unable to prove. The fact, now well known, that elliptical trajectories with the Sun at a focus necessitate a central force proportional to the inverse square of the radius vector, required for its proof the use of infinitesimal calculus. This had, of course, to await Newton and his fluxions.

But the age of reason was already heralding its triumph—and Kepler himself, a pious soul but averse to all theological disputes, sounds its clarion call in the introduction to his *New Astronomy*, which proclaimed proudly the independence of science from theology.

'. . . As regards the opinions of the saints about the matters of nature, I answer in one word: that in theology the weight of Authority, but in philosophy the weight of Reason is to be considered. Therefore, a saint was Lactantius, who denied the rotundity of the Earth; a saint was Augustine, who admitted the rotundity, but denied the existence of the antipodes. Sacred is the Holy Office of our day, which admits the smallness of the Earth but denies its motion: but to me more sacred than all these is Truth, which leads me, with all respect for the doctors of the Church, to demonstrate from philosophy that the Earth is round, circumhabited by antipodes, of a most insignificant smallness, and in a word, belongs among the Planets'.

If we compare these stirring words with the timid and truly medieval petulousness of Copernicus transpiring from the quotations reproduced on p. 50, we shall appreciate more fully the distance which the avant-garde of scientific opinion of that time travelled in the intervening seventy years.

And the *Astronomia Nova*—the scientific masterpiece of Johannes Kepler, and the basis of his claim to immortality—deserves our admiration and sympathy also for other reasons. Like Ptolemy's *Almagest*, Copernicus's *De Revolutionibus* or Newton's *Principia,* Kepler's *Astronomia Nova* was written in Latin, then still the universal language of the scholars, and Kepler was not only easily the best writer of this illustrious company, but also the most sincere; and his sincerity has opened for us a unique insight into the working of a truly great mind. Copernicus's book, written in a turgid and unimaginative style, never found many readers; throughout centuries it has remained one of those works which everyone praised from hearsay, but which few bothered to read. Not so with Kepler: his *Astronomia Nova* represented, in fact, almost a scientific diary of his heroic years 1602–1604, faithfully recording all twists and turns of the creative process that resulted in the birth of modern astronomy with a disarming frankness that has no equal in the annals of our science, and which the reader can judge for himself from the quotations we have reproduced in this text. Newton, with his secretive inclination, took pains to erase all signs of his creative processes, before agreeing reluctantly to disclose their results long after the creative fire had gone. He also shared with Copernicus his peculiar aversion to acknowledging help which they received from others. In this respect, Johannes

Kepler could serve as an endearing example of generosity—to his masters, as well as contemporaries and successors alike.

Indeed, there was nothing of a schemer or an 'operator' in him seeking self-advancement in fields other than science through his scientific efforts—features which mar the historical image of both Galileo or Newton, and which did not become extinct by any means among their successors. Neither the example of Tycho, nor the high position in which he succeeded him, turned Kepler's head or soiled his pure soul. When Michael Mästlin, Kepler's teacher from his Tübingen years, congratulated his former pupil on his appointment to the post of Imperial Mathematician, Kepler replied (in a letter written in 1604) with disarming frankness: 'High honours or distinctions do not exist in my eyes. I live here [i.e., in Prague] on the stage of the world as a private person; and when I manage to squeeze out of the Court at least a part of my salary, I am glad that I do not have to live entirely from my own. Besides, I so conduct myself as though I were serving, not only the Emperor, but all mankind in its posterity. With a secret pride, stemming from this hope, I look with disdain on all worldly honours or distinctions; and often also on those who dispense them. As the only favour vouchsafed to me by Divine Providence I recognise the fact that I gained access to Tycho's observations.' A truly 'angelic doctrine', as his contemporary Galileo Galilei would have muttered with tongue in cheek, but which he would have been far from willing to follow. In fact, for ages to come we shall meet no one quite like Kepler in this respect—until, perhaps, in the 20th century in the person of another one of Kepler's fellow-Swabians: Albert Einstein.

The date of publication of Kepler's *Astronomia Nova* (together with the almost simultaneous discovery of the telescope) made the years 1609–1610 the veritable watershed in the history of astronomy, a dividing line between ancient times and the modern epoch. They also mark the culminating point in Kepler's life, both scientific and personal. For since the death, in 1612, of his imperial patron Rudolph II, Kepler found his position at the Court in Prague increasingly uncertain, and the drain on the imperial exchequer caused by demands of the state, made payment of his salary more and more irregular. Therefore, in response to the exigencies of daily life Kepler sought, and obtained, permission from the new monarch, Matthias, to accept temporarily the post of Provincial Mathematician at Linz in Upper Austria, where he was to spend the next fifteen years of his life. In 1612, in the deepening shadow of the gathering storm which, a few years later, was to tear Europe asunder as the Thirty Years' War, Kepler left Prague where he had spent the best years of his life. He was accompanied by the fame of being the first astronomer of his time, but left behind the graves of his first wife Barbara (née Müller) and of his son.

Kepler's first marriage and the latter years of his family life had their share of shadows and misfortunes, reflected in the following excerpts from a letter which, after the death of Frau Barbara, Kepler sent to a lady—we do not know her name—whose hand he was wooing (without success):

'The well-born, noble, virtuous and very gracious Lady', he wrote. 'There is nothing bad about astronomy. An astronomer is far better than as artisan or a merchant, and is held in greater esteem than a teacher. He makes a better husband than a clergyman. His status is rather like that of a physician, but more highly regarded if he has got his income. . . . If God gave my late wife better health of body and soul, and to me a steadier income so that she would have had both means and inclination to move in society, I know of no reason why my astronomy should have been any drawback to her. I never heard anyone calling her Mrs. Stargazer—except, perhaps, jokingly. She was always called by my name. . . . .

'. . . Well, then, I am a Mathematician, Philosopher, and Historian. Out of thousands very few know the full scope of these terms. This great land on Ems (Upper Austria) appointed me under these terms as their official. They need a scientist who is widely read, remembers much, and can use it for the benefit of his employers. Mathematics is concerned with all that can be measured and computed; philosophy with the cause of things, and with good manners or honest behaviour. It is also concerned with reasonable means for happier conduct of our fragile life. History is concerned with past events of the State and Church; and also with all teachings of the past. If preachers today would observe them better, there would be less strife among them. Astronomy is but a part of mathematics. This, then, is the service I render to my King, and am styled a Mathematician. I have been entrusted with the publication of a famous book to honour the late Emperor Rudolph, of which the

Book of David in the 19th Psalm speaks: "The Heavens declare the Glory of the Lord." These titles are sufficient for me. . . .'

But returning to the subject of his first wife, Kepler goes on with his painful confession;

'. . . Secondly, it was declared in my disfavour that I did not treat my late wife well, especially that I tormented her with high-sounding matters. I answer this calumny by saying that in our whole life together I never even laid a finger upon her, or ever offended her with an angry word; nor had she ever need to complain of my infidelity. My conscience is clear and confident in the testimony of all our acquaintances that she always praised me for my honest care; for I esteemed her in all possible ways and loved her truly.

'God willed it, however, that my salary was not always regularly paid, while my wife grew ill and melancholy. This often depressed her; and during such depressions she would not allow me to touch her property, nor even to pawn a single cup—as though I should want to reduce her to misery. I cannot deny having been sorely vexed time and again over her needless stinginess, and more than once was moved to reproach her in angry words. And because her illness entailed a gradual loss of memory, my reminders and admonishments frequently upset her; for although she was incapable of independent action, she resented advice. . . . It is true that I showed often impatience when she either could not remember something, or was again inquiring about everything. But I never called her a fool, although she probably sensed that I considered her to be of simple mind; for she was very sensitive. Altogether there was much bitterness and anger between us, but this never degenerated into enmity; for basically we knew that our hearts felt for each other.

'Thirdly, allegations have been raised that I hold strange ideas about religion—half Papist, half Calvinist. My answer to the charge of heterodoxy is that the preachers in their pulpits are presuming too much, and do not wish to retain old-fashioned simplicity. They indulge in needless disputation, and introduce novelties which are at variance with the true piety. They falsely accuse each other, inflame quarrels among the Dukes and Earls. They testify to many evils about Papists, and these will cause the defection of many when persecution returns again. I am confident to speak of these matters because, as a young man, I made a vow to study them;

and read more about them than many a preacher. This is, however, of no concern to simple people. No honest man will ever assert that I have tried to trouble my wife or children with these matters in the least, or lead them to read strange books. This can be attested by the priest from whom I receive my communion.'

The text of this letter of rare sincerity offers an eloquent insight into Kepler's life and times. It portrays in perspective a sad end of his married life with his first wife—a life which commenced so auspiciously only ten years before. Although the anonymous lady to whom the foregoing letter was addressed did not become (perhaps not surprisingly) Kepler's second wife—that fate was eventually reserved for Johanna Reuttinger, by many years Kepler's junior, who also outlived him—the text of the letter leaves no room for doubt that Frau Barbara developed with time into a neurotic whose passing must have been a redemption for her as well as her sorely tried husband; and that the irascible Brahe, the melancholy and withdrawn Emperor Rudolph II, or the egocentric condottiere Wallenstein were not the only unusual personalities with whom Kepler had to contend in the course of his life.

Kepler's principal scientific achievement at Linz was the publication, in 1618, of his *Harmonices Mundi*, containing the statement of the third (and last) of his famous planetary laws: namely, the one stating that the squares of the orbital periods of the planets bear the same ratio to each other as the cubes of the semi-major axes of their elliptical orbits. That Kepler was fully aware of the significance of his three laws and of the vistas opening up to astronomy in the future, was expressed movingly by him on that occasion.

'Eighteen months ago, the first dawn rose for me, three months ago, the bright day, and a few days ago, the full sun of a most wonderful vision; now nothing can keep me back. I let myself go in divine exultation. I defy the mortals with scorn by an open confession. I have stolen the golden vessels of the Egyptians to make out of them a holy tabernacle for my God—far away from the frontiers of Egypt. If you pardon me, I shall be delighted; should you be angry, I shall bear it. Well then, the die is cast. I am writing this book for my contemporaries or—what does it matter?—for posterity. Has not God himself waited six thousand years for someone to contemplate his work with understanding?'

After that, there was only one more achievement worthy of the great astronomer, on which Kepler worked with indefatigable zeal, the completion of the tables of the planetary positions, based on his new laws of their motion. This task occupied him for the next nine years, while the religious intolerance, no smaller among the Protestants than between the Catholics and Protestants, and other vicissitudes of the times forced him to change his assistants, his printer and even his own abode several times.

During the last years of his life—while the Thirty Years' War, which broke out in Prague in 1618, continued to ravage Central Europe—he wandered like a comet through the Imperial lands, in quest of a new temporary haven or a new patron willing to engage the Imperial Mathematician for pay as an astrologer. This pre-occupation, dangerous in times of war, also brought him into temporary contact with Wallenstein, and at times gave rise to despondency from which he tried to emerge by contemplation of the heavenly wonders. 'When the storms are raging and the ship-wreck of state is threatening us', wrote Kepler to his son-in-law, Jacob Bartsch, on November 6th, 1629, 'there is nothing nobler for us to be done than to let down the anchor of our peaceful studies into the ground of eternity'.

The planetary tables, published at last at Ulm in 1627 under the title of *Tabulae Rudolphinae* (in honour of his first benevolent patron) represented the last great achievement of Kepler's life, for his earthly days were by then really numbered. When he saw that he could no longer place his hopes in Wallenstein's goodwill or luck, he took to the road again in the fall of 1630, to see whether he could receive the salary due to him as Imperial Mathematician and its arrears from the Reichstag, then meeting in Regensburg. Kepler, now already an old man, waged a long trip from Silesia, via Leipzig, to Bavaria on horseback. This last trip of this astronomer of world fame, riding through half of Germany on a worn-out jade (which he sold, on arrival, for two gulden) hunting for a salary earned many years before, has remained unique in the annals of the history of astronomy, and was an act of incomparable pathos.

The great exertions of this trip, in the fog and storms of November weather in Central Europe, brought Kepler to Regensburg as a man sick unto death; and he died there, after a short illness, on November 15th of 1630, not quite sixty years of age. The funeral procession of the great astronomer was—so the chronicles say—attended by many members of that illustrious Diet as Kepler was laid to rest in the Protestant cemetery of St. Peter's outside the towns' walls. Only three years later this whole cemetery with Kepler's tomb was, however, completely laid waste during the conquest of the city by the Duke Bernhard of Weimar in the turmoil of the Thirty Years' War, so that no one knows today the final resting place of his earthly remains. But the Promethean light which his life-long efforts have brought us down to the Earth will for ever remain an integral part of our science.

In surveying, from the retrospect of more than three centuries, Kepler's principal contributions to astronomical science, we must also mention, however, what he has *not* done; because some of it concerns intimately the subject of his book: and that is to enlarge the size of the solar system to realistic dimensions. The immortal achievement of Johannes Kepler has been to liberate the solar-system astronomy from the 'epistomological trash' of the Pythagoreans and complicated geometry of the eccentrics and epicycles, with which it was infested by Ptolemy or Copernicus. This he did through his first and second laws of planetary motion. Moreover, through his third law, Kepler provided us with an exact means of determining the proportional sizes of planetary orbits in terms of the orbital periods (which can be ascertained from observations with great accuracy), and thus obtaining an accurate model of the solar system. But how about its absolute dimensions?

To this question, in truth, Kepler could give only an answer still largely borrowed from the ancients. In his last work—*Somnium, sive Astronomia Lunaris*—published posthumously in 1634, Kepler confessed that, in his early versions he 'was still agreeing with the ancient authorities that the Sun was about 1200 Earth radii distant from the Earth; the Moon, about 60 radii', leading to a 20:1 ratio of the sizes of the orbits of the Earth and the Moon. In his *Rudolphine Tables* (1627) and the final (posthumous) version of the *Somnium*, Kepler increased this ratio rather arbitrarily to 60:1. The unit of length, the Earth-Moon distance, was adopted by Kepler as being sixty times as large as the radius of the terrestrial globe (a very good estimate, but still largely taken over from the ancients). But the 60:1 ratio for the Earth:Moon orbit rendered the solar system only three times larger than the value adopted for it in antiquity, and still only about one-seventh of the actual size!

One wonders, in particular, how it was possible that observers like Tycho Brahe could still be satisfied with the results of the triangulation of the Sun-Earth-Moon system which came down from Aristarchos in the 3rd century B.C.? With his observational skill (and knowledge of refraction) Tycho could have improved the ancient value considerably, and established a more realistic estimate of the dimensions of the solar system. For reasons which are difficult now to recapture, the problem failed to attract his attention, and astronomers had to await for its solution almost until the end of the century which commenced with the year of Tycho's death.

Before, however, we come to that part of our story, we must make our acquaintance with the other Founding Father of modern astronomy at the beginning of the 17th century—Galileo Galilei—and with his magic 'optic tube', which was so profoundly to influence our science ever after.

GALILEO GALILEI: Beginning of Telescopic Astronomy

Galileo Galilei (1564–1642) the second Founding Father of modern astronomy, was seven years old when Kepler was born, and outlived him by twelve years. Chance willed it that the year of his death was also the one of the birth of Isaac Newton (1642–1727) —thus were the lives of all three intertwined. Although, therefore, Galileo was the oldest of the three, he does not enter the narrative proper of this book until relatively late in his life; and his contact with our subject has remained much more accidental (though no less dramatic) than was the case with Kepler. That is why we have relegated him in the arrangement of our text to the second place.

Galileo Galilei was born on 5th February 1564 in Pisa, of a family of impoverished Florentine nobility which had taken to commerce. He received an excellent education at the Jesuit school of the Monastery of Vallombrosa (near Florence) and later at the University of Pisa, though he seems to have left the latter without any degree. His discovery, in 1589, of the isochronism of a pendulum (i.e., of the fact that the time in which a pendulum swings back and forth depends only on its length, and not on the amplitude of swing) opened up for him the way to an early academic career at the age of 25 — first at Pisa, and three years later (1592) at Padua, where he was to spend, as professor of mathematics, the next eighteen years. Although this time covered the best years of his life (corresponding to Kepler's years in Prague), he published nothing then of any consequence; his growing reputation rested largely on his lectures, and partly on simple mechanical inventions (such as a thermoscope, or proportional compass) which he manufactured with hired artisans in his workshop.

Galileo was not destined to rise from local renown to European fame until almost the age of 46, and the circumstances of this rise are intimately connected with another discovery which was not initially his own, but which he was the first one to turn to the sky: namely, the telescope.

The story of the discovery of the telescope remains still shrouded in a bit of a mystery which does not lack elements of the dramatic. Whatever we may think now of the cryptic indications contained in the earlier sources from the end of the 16th century, it is certain that towards the end of the first decade of the 17th century telescopes suddenly appeared in several places of Western Europe, such as Middelburgh in Holland, or Paris in France. Whether their appearance was due to independent discoveries, or news of it rapidly spreading from one source, is very difficult to fathom at this time.

Was it the reported appearance of the telescope at the Rialto in Venice in the spring of 1609, or the news received by Galileo from Paris which drew his attention to this wonderful device? Whatever happened, we know that soon thereafter he was able to construct 'cannocchiales' (yet to be named a telescope) of his own making which were optically superior to all others, and, what is more, he turned them to the heavens. Although he may not have been actually the first to do so (there are reports of contemporary observations of the Moon by Thomas Harriot in England, or of Jupiter's satellites by Simon Mayer in Germany), Galileo scored his early observational triumphs not only by the skill of his hands, but mainly by the fact that his mind was prepared to accept what his eyes saw; and this entitled him to be truly considered as the father of telescopic astronomy.

It must indeed have been an enchanted time — those autumn and winter months of 1609–10 at Padua—when the human eye for the first time beheld so many heavenly wonders; and how we regret that Galileo was not endowed with the pen (and pure soul) of a Kepler to recapture them for us as the great Swabian would have done in his place! For when Galileo got around to writing up his early telescopic discoveries in his famous tract *Nuncius Sidereus* (Venice, 1610) what came out was a sober, matter-of-fact account of the events and a description of the observations—which could almost pass for publication in any one of our contemporary scientific journals. Thus even in the matter of presentation Galileo has proved, more than Kepler, to be a precursor of modern times. Just as modern theoretical astronomy was born with the publication of Kepler's *Astronomia Nova* in the summer of 1609, Galileo's *Nuncius Sidereus* in the spring of 1610 heralded the advent of telescopic observations. It is these two milestones which mark, almost simultaneously, the watershed in time between the ancient and modern astronomy. In the first part of this chapter we followed one of its sources entering into rapids from which astronomy was to emerge as one mighty stream following its course towards more distant goals; now we shall describe the other.

'Oh, much-knowing perspicil', exclaimed Kepler around that time 'more precious than any sceptre! He who holds thee in his right hand is a true king, a world ruler . . .' So Galileo beheld it in his hand during those enchanted summer and autumn nights at Padua in 1609, and gasped in awe. The Moon, when viewed with a magnification that brought it to an apparent distance of two terrestrial diameters, proved to possess a surface that is . . . 'neither smooth nor uniform, . . . but uneven, rough, replete with cavities and packed with protruding eminences, in no other wise than the Earth with its mountains and valleys'; and the scientist in Galileo was already estimating the heights of the lunar mountains from the length of the shadows cast by them at the time of lunar sunrise or sunset.

During the dark of the Moon periods Galileo watched the stars, and found a great many more of them than could be seen with the naked eye—especially in the direction of the Milky Way. More important still, increasing the magnification did not increase the size of the stellar image seen through the telescope. Tycho Brahe must have been deceived by appearances when he assigned to the

Fig. 11.   **GALILEO GALILEI**
(1564–1642)

"Eppur si muove"
(A portrait by Giusto Sustermans by courtesy of the Ronan Picture Library).

stars apparent diameters measured in angular minutes; the telescope showed them to be immeasurably small.

But the greatest surprise awaited Galileo in the first weeks of the
year 1610, when the planet Jupiter was approaching opposition.
On the 7th January Galileo saw, to his amazement, Jupiter to be
attended by three little starlets, and on 13th January he noted a
fourth. Moreover, repeated observations on successive nights left
no room for doubt that these objects revolved around Jupiter in
the same plane, and with orbital periods of less than two days to
more than two weeks. Here was a model of the solar system in
miniature! Galileo could wait no longer. He rapidly wrote up a
brief and factual account of his observations (the latest of which
was dated March 2nd), and already on March 13th the first copies of
his *Nuncius Sidereus* left Baglioni's printing shop in Venice to
spread the heavenly message among those who cared to read it.
Kepler's *Astronomia Nova*, which appeared nine month's before,
constitutes an ageless monument towering like a granitic obelisk
over contemporary astronomical literature; but its text is as difficult
to follow in places as ancient hieroglyphs. In contrast, Galileo's
Nuncius is written in an almost terse, matter-of-fact style reminiscent of Caesar's *Commentaries* or modern high-school English.

When we thus pause today to peruse this little tract which
heralded the advent of modern astronomy, we are driven to the conclusion that Galileo was not of the stuff of which great observers
are made. His drawings of the Moon show no detail which we could
safely recognise today, nor is it possible to identify the positions of
the eighty odd stars which he described in the region of Orion's belt,
and his drawings of the Pleiades are likewise largely enigmatic.
Even when we take account of the haste with which his booklet
must have been composed, we cannot escape the conclusion that
Galileo was not a born astronomical observer—a conclusion
supported also by the fact that his interest in observations lasted
only a very short time. In 1611, after Galileo returned from
Padua to Florence, he was still to discover the phases of Venus
('Mater amorum aemulatur Cynthiae formas') and he thought he
also noted a phase effect in the shape of the apparent disc of Mars.
But, apart from subsequent observation of the peculiar form of
the planet Saturn—a puzzle which was eventually resolved by the
discovery of Saturn's rings in 1655–1656 by Christiaan Huyghens

—Galileo made no further telescopic discoveries, or observations of any note. Indeed, his brief encounter with observational astronomy seems to have been limited only to the years 1609–1611. By that time he still had more than thirty years to live, and his eyesight (which failed him towards the end) remained long unimpaired. We are, therefore, driven to the conclusion that the real cause why his astronomical career was cut so short must have been a loss of interest. By the skill of his hands and experimental bent of mind Galileo certainly exceeded Kepler; but as an observer—in comparison with a man like Brahe—he was an amateur.

How did Galileo rank as a theoretician and cosmologist? Before the impact of his telescopic discoveries, Galileo was at best a crypto-Copernican. He was acquainted with the idea of a heliocentric planetary system, and in his first letter to Kepler (dated August 4th, 1597) he proclaimed himself an adherent of Copernicus —in private, but not in public. For the text of his lectures is still extant in which he not only taught his students in Padua the old astronomy according to Ptolemy up to at least 1606, but in which he also expressly repudiated Copernicus by conventional Aristotelian arguments worthy of an academic backwoodsman.

However, Galileo's telescopic discoveries of 1609–1611 have worked their magic, and a former crypto-Copernican becomes firmly convinced of the truth of the heliocentric system. In point of fact, since that time till the fateful year of 1633 when he was muzzled by the Inquisition, Galileo seems to have made the propaganda of the Copernican astronomy and of the double motion of the Earth—diurnal as well as annual—the central goal of his life. Although the ensuing historical tragedy which culminated in the catastrophe of 1633 was principally one of the fallibility of human nature—both of Galileo and of his adversaries—its secular repercussions necessitate that we consider briefly its roots, and attempt to reassess its historical significance for the subsequent evolution of astronomy, taking advantage of all the benefits of hindsight.

When Galileo first beheld in the autumn of 1610 that the planet Venus exhibited a 'horned disc' the size of which varied with the phase, and with its illuminated part always facing the Sun—an easy observation, soon confirmed and generally accepted by others— did it prove that Venus must revolve around the Sun rather than the Earth? Not necessarily so; for our Moon exhibits similar phases in solar illumination, and yet it revolves around the Earth. However, in the orbit of Venus as constructed by Ptolemy, this planet could only appear as a *crescent* to us (on account of the fact that it never deviates more than 48° from the Sun at maximum elongations) in the telescope. It was Galileo's discovery that Venus exhibits also *gibbous* phases in the course of its orbital cycle that proved it to be in heliocentric orbit. This fact, by itself, spelt the final doom of the Ptolemaic picture of the solar system. It was accepted as such, not only by laymen, but also by the leading authorities of the Jesuit Collegium in Rome—Fathers Clavius or Grienberger—of that time.

Did it, however, necessarily make Copernicus right? By no means; for the same phenomena would be expected also on the basis of the ancient theory of Heracleides, revived more recently by Tycho Brahe, according to which all planets indeed revolved round the Sun, but together with the Sun around the Earth. This model would equally 'save' all phenomena observed by Galileo, and, to this extent, the four satellites revolving around Jupiter could constitute an analogy of the solar system without the Earth. All phenomena actually observed could, in fact, be just as well formally accounted for without upsetting the Earth on its cosmic pedestal and setting it in motion. This was the next 'line of defence' of Aristotelian physics to which the academic backwoodsmen of the day were willing to retreat brandishing their stone axes; but not Galileo. His instinct of a physicist convinced him that the Tychonic system with its ancient pedigree constituted only a fictitious makeshift devised mainly to suit the opinions of the theologians, and in this he was, of course, right. Kepler the mathematician arrived at the same conclusion, and at an even earlier time. The tragedy of Galileo Galilei goes back to the fact that he was, however, unable to *prove* what he came so passionately to believe, by arguments which would satisfy him and convince others.

Moreover, in this quest he singularly failed to grasp the helping hand stretched out to him by Kepler across the Alps—that Kepler who in his *Dissertatio cum Nuncio Sidereo* (1610) offered to act as Galileo's shield-bearer in the service of the common cause. In the end, in his *Dialogues on the Two Great World Systems* (Ptolemaic and Copernican—the Tychonic he ignored altogether), Galileo resorted to argumentation or special pleading which was not only incorrect in places, but downright phoney—so phoney that it is difficult for us to see how Galileo could have believed himself what he wrote. Did his critical sense get blunted by the years so that he did not perceive the internal contradictions of some of his arguments; or did he, in the Jesuit spirit that 'ends sanctify the means', take his reader knowingly for a ride? Historians of science disagree in their opinions, and we may never know for sure.

What was the main purpose of the *Dialogues,* which in 1633 brought such a storm over Galileo's head? To prove the motion of the Earth; and the principal reason which Galileo produced in favour of this view during the 'fourth day' of the *Dialogues* through the mouth of Salviati, were the *tides.* This was, as we know, an entirely erroneous concept, for the oceanic tides are in reality caused by luni-solar attraction. Moreover, Galileo cannot even be absolved by the excuse that the underlying theory of gravitation was still ahead of his time. The empirical connection between the position of the Moon in the sky and the height of the tides was noticed by Pytheas of Massilia in the 2nd half of the 4th century B.C., or Seleucus of Chaldea about a hundred years later; and, in Galileo's own time, Kepler developed this concept to a considerable extent in his *Astronomia Nova.* Galileo was vaguely aware of Kepler's views, but dismissed them disdainfully as an 'astrological superstition'. In actual fact, the mathematician Kepler, guided by the observations, was groping slowly (and remarkably closely) towards the theory of universal gravitation soon to be installed as the guiding spirit of dynamical astronomy. But Galileo the physicist and philosopher had still no inkling of it until the end of his days.

And worse than that. What Galileo set out to champion in his *Dialogues* with such dialectic skill was the Copernican astronomy of vintage 1543, with all its cobwebs of epicyclic paraphernalia. Galileo had, in fact, much greater justification to call himself a Copernican than Kepler who proved to be a much greater innovator than Copernicus, though he continued to call himself his disciple out of a sense of innate generosity. In particular, throughout his life Galileo remained completely under the spell of the ancient Pythagorean lore that motions of all celestial bodies must be uniform and circular. In this he found himself to be a strange bedfellow of all his Aristotelian adversaries. When Prince Cesi, founder of the Italian *Accademia dei Lincei* and one of Galileo's benevolent patrons, said that he would gladly favour the Copernican system if it could be divested of its eccentrics and epicycles, Galileo replied (in a letter of 30 June, 1612): 'If anyone wants to deny the epicycles, he must deny the paths of the satellites of Jupiter . . . Eccentrics exist; for what else is the path of Mars according to the best observations?' And this three years after Kepler published *Astronomia Nova*!

Most biographers of Kepler have been irritated by Galileo's obtuseness in matters of cosmology, while the admirers of Galileo find it difficult to conceal their embarrassment. For although *Astronomia Nova* was on Galileo's desk from 1609 (he received a 'complimentary copy' from Kepler), its contents seem to have been completely ignored by Galileo, for whom planetary orbits remained circles until the end of his life. How do we account for this 'blind spot' of Galileo's? His lame remark that '. . . His (i.e., Kepler's) way of doing philosophy is not mine' surely does not contain the whole truth—which we shall not find unless we dig deeper below the superficial meaning of his words. And we do not, perhaps, need to dig very far before the naked truth will stare us in the face: namely, that Galileo missed completely the fundamental significance of Kepler's contributions because he failed to understand them.

We should remember in this connection, that, unlike Kepler, who was 'the astronomer's astronomer', fully versed in all aspects of the contemporary state of the art, Galileo never became a properly accredited member of the fraternity. The extant texts of his Paduan lectures disclose the hand of an inspiring physicist, but only a run-of-the-mill astronomer of rather mediocre mathematical skill or knowledge. On the other hand, we must admit that Kepler's masterpiece was written in a discursive style, which made considerable demands on the reader's patience as well as knowledge. There is no evidence that the 46-year old Galileo possessed this patience, or ever made any real effort to understand what Kepler had to say between the covers of his book. But vain and conceited as he became in the wake of his telescopic discoveries between 1609–1611, and full of concern about his 'image' in the eyes of his contemporaries, how could he confess it without loss of face; and how could he cover it up except by studied silence? Galileo is not the first man of science we have met in our narrative to camouflage his predicament with this strategy, nor have men like this become extinct since. The type is indeed well known in our time, and about as abundant as men of Kepler's candour are rare.

These rather obvious deductions should go a long way towards explaining the peculiar relations—or, rather, the lack of them—between the two Founding Fathers of our science during their lifetimes; and such evidence as there is in this respect does not tend to place Galileo's person in too good a light. Johannes Kepler—a man blessed far less by good fortune than his Italian contemporary —with all his virtues and some shortcomings, stands truly on the watershed between ancient astronomy and modern times. While, by his science, he was a precursor of the future, medieval elements in his personality were still strong; and at his best, he is ageless. Not so Galileo, whose attitude towards the past was one of contempt; towards the future, largely of indifference; but of lively interest for the blessings of the day.

A historian who delves more closely into the facts of Galileo's life for which we have no room in this book—into his efforts in 1610 to use the telescope, not only (or even mainly) for astronomical observations, but also as an instrument of self-advancement; in which he played the Venetian Republic and the Court of Tuscany skilfully against each other in quest of material benefits for himself and his family; into Galileo's endless quarrels with his contemporaries motivated largely by personal conceit ('You cannot deny, Mr. Sarsi' [the pseudonym for the Jesuit Father Horatio Grassi, used in Galileo's tract *Il Saggiatore*] 'that it was granted to me alone to discover all the new phenomena in the sky, and nothing to anybody else') which eclipsed by far the egocentrism of Tycho Brahe; into Galileo's ability to camouflage by cleverness or sarcasm the lack of real knowledge, and, above all, into an almost total absence of any contemplative leanings at a time emerging from the Middle Ages, coupled with a predominant concern for temporal interests—will see in front of him a person much more akin to the professional 'operators' of our time than to his contemporary Kepler, who was still half steeped in medieval mystics. As a personality, Galileo does not, therefore, stand astride the watershed between ancient and modern ways of life; he is already wholly and frighteningly modern.

Indeed, we could apply to Galileo the same words by which one of the British Astronomers Royal of Victorian times was described by a recent historian of science: 'He . . . divided the people around him into two groups: those who had succeeded and were worthy of cultivation; and those who had not succeeded and were beneath notice'. For, we are afraid, Galileo's actions showed only too clearly that he would have classified Kepler into the second category: for who would cultivate a man who cannot even exact a salary from his employer? No one would have been allowed to play such a trick on Galileo and get away with it. Even the stipend bestowed upon him by the Pope Urban VIII in the days of his glory was not withdrawn from him after his condemnation by the Inquisition!

It we look back at Galileo's work and try to assess the main cosmological objectives of his scientific life after more than three centuries which separate us from his time, in what light do they appear to us today? In the main objectives of his advocacy—the diurnal as well as annual motion of the Earth—Galileo was, of course, right. None of the principal arguments he adduced in favour of his views could, however, stand the light of subsequent scrutiny, and were rapidly forgotten by all but the historians of science. Kepler had no more luck either, but he did not concern himself (in this particular instance) too much with the causes, as with a phenomenological description. This brought him within an ace of the discovery of the role of universal gravitation eighty years before Newton, while Galileo—the founder of modern mechanics—was blinded by his obsession with tides from getting any glimpse of it. He could follow with acute reasoning the path of a stone thrown by human hand, or of a projectile shot from a gun; but his reason did not yet cross the distance to the Moon to realise that the Moon describes a similar trajectory around the Earth. For this, we had to await the advent of Newton.

What are the proofs of the actual double motion of the Earth which would be satisfactory to the physicist today? For the annual motion around the Sun, the aberration of light (see next chapter); while for the diurnal motion, the rotation of the plane of a swinging pendulum. As regards the latter, it almost seems as though Nature—that most delightful of teasers—intended to play a gentle joke on Galileo Galilei. The reader may recall that the first claim to fame of young Galileo was his discovery of the isochronism of a pendulum, which he made, according to tradition, in watching the long cantilever of Pisa Cathedral swing gently during divine services. Now if only Galileo was as devout a soul as he later professed to be and spent more of his time in the church (or if the services had lasted longer), would it have been too much to hope that he could have noticed the plane of the swing *change orientation* as time went on?

This would have confirmed the axial rotation of the Earth, one of the theses which Galileo tried so passionately to prove later in his life. Yet he failed to make this observation which Nature dangled teasingly in front of his eyes, and thus missed his chance. Actually, this experiment—staged in 1851 by Foucault in the dome of the Pantheon in Paris—would have required rational mechanics for its interpretation, for which we have to await the time of Euler (1707–1783). Yet, perhaps, a flash of genius could have enabled Galileo to divine the actual cause of the phenomenon, just as Kepler divined the existence of gravitation as the force responsible for the motion of the planets, long before this could be proved by Newton. At any rate, this flash failed to materialise, and Galileo went through the rest of his life convinced of the Earth's diurnal motion, but unable to prove it.

As regards the Earth's annual motion around the Sun, Galileo deserves a more honourable mention, for his indirect contributions to its eventual proof. This proof, represented by the phenomenon of aberration, is based on the fact that the velocity with which the Earth orbits around the Sun, 30 km/sec (18.6 mls/sec) is a finite fraction of the velocity of the propagation of light. This fact gives, in turn, rise to an apparent yearly motion of the positions of fixed stars, detected first by Bradley in 1728, almost a century after Galileo's time. Kepler (in his *Ad Vitellionem Parallipomena* of 1604) still held the velocity of light to be infinite, in which case there would be no aberration. On the other hand, Galileo not only admitted that light could propagate with a finite speed, but proposed also a simple method for measuring it. Although his attempts to do so could not have been expected to lead to significant results, the first realistic determination of the speed with which light propagates through space was carried out by Olaf Roemer in 1676, on the basis of the 'light equation' in the times of the eclipses of the satellites of Jupiter discovered by Galileo in 1610. To this extent Galileo can at least claim the right of grand parentage. He did not discover it, but laid down foundations to the road which eventually led to discovery; and this should be noted to his credit side, to offset some of the specious arguments advanced in his *Dialogues*. Like the evolution of the species, evolution of thought does not often take shortcuts: it is rather apt to meander around often in an almost haphazard fashion, and the lives of the two Founding Fathers of modern astronomy—Kepler as well as Galileo—offer ample examples of this process.

THE TIME OF NEWTON: Mensuration of the Solar System

With the close of the first third of the 17th century, we are entering a period which shall take us without further detours to modern times. The eggs of modern cosmology were laid by the two of its Founding Fathers around 1610, yet their time of hatching extended well over the next fifty years or more, until the time of Isaac Newton (1642–1727), who brought them out to full life.

Isaac Newton, the third Founding Father of our science, whose personality dominates the second half of the 17th century like Kepler and Galileo did in the first, was born in the year when Galileo died, and outlived his life span by eight years. It is impossible to give in this short chapter even a brief account of all the contributions by which his versatile genius enriched our science; and most of them are not concerned directly with the subject of this book. His central contribution was, of course, a mathematical proof of the fact that planetary orbits are direct consequences of solar attraction, varying as the inverse square of the distance. In more specific terms, the description of the planetary motions embodied in Kepler's laws represented nothing else but closed integrals of the 'problem of two bodies', moving in an inverse-square force field.

Kepler discovered these 'integrals' empirically by a careful analysis of Tycho's observations; but Newton was the first to recognise in these laws the necessary consequence of a universal 'law of gravitation', according to which any two bodies attract each other by a force which is directly proportional to the product of their mass, and inversely proportional to the square of their distance. In other words, while the true geometry of the solar system was first recognised by Kepler, it was Newton who identified the spring of its mechanical clockwork with universal gravity.

Not that Newton was the first to consider the idea of the gravity itself. Johannes Kepler, in his *Astronomia Nova* (1609) conjectured that the driving force which moves the planets in their orbits emanated from the Sun (Kepler compared it with 'magnetism'); and, in one place, even ventured an opinion that it varies with the inverse square of the distance—only to discard this idea a little later. The idea did, however, flicker around and 'hung in the air'— shyly at first, but later with increasing insistency. It was in the mind of Robert Hooke (1635–1703), an older contemporary of Newton; and Newton may, in fact, have heard of it first from Hooke. However, no one before Newton was able to prove that Kepler's laws of planetary motions were necessary consequences of an inverse-square force field. This proof had to await the advent of the infinitesimal calculus, and this was discovered independently by Leibnitz. The latter was, however, a pure mathematician, not interested much in astronomy or the physical world. Newton was, on the contrary, an 'applied mathematician' par excellence, interested in solving concrete problems. His solution of the 'problem of two bodies' constitutes his central contribution to astronomy, and one which through his work and that of his successors, from Euler, Lagrange, Gauss and Poincaré—to name only the greatest—eventually earned for celestial mechanics a pre-eminence unequalled by any other branch of human science.

But although Newton was the towering scientific personality of his age, whose impact profoundly influenced subsequent developments in many branches of astronomy, other developments were taking place which affected more directly the main subject of this book: namely, our knowledge of the size of the Universe in which we live. Moreover, these developments no longer grew out of isolated efforts of single individuals, but originated with groups of scientists whose work was sponsored by public authority. For the second half of the 17th century saw the foundation in Western Europe of the first permanent observatories set up to conduct systematic astronomical observations—such as the Royal Observatories of Paris (founded in 1667) in France, or Royal Greenwich Observatory (founded in 1675) in England; institutions which carry on their distinguished traditions up to the present time.

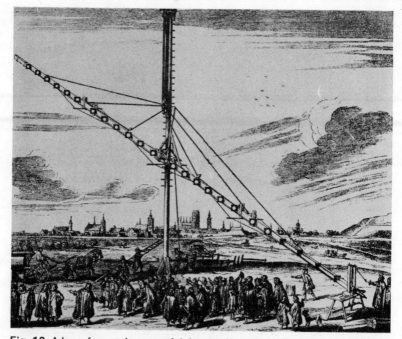

Fig. 12. A long-focus telescope of Johannes Hevelius in Danzig around 1650—a representative example of the era of telescopic Dinosaurs carrying small heads on long necks (long focus being chosen to minimise chromatic aberration of their simple objectives).

And, moreover, in 1666 King Louis XIV founded the French Academy to serve as a Government advisory body in scientific matters and to promote the growth of useful knowledge in which astronomy was fully included. While the Royal Society founded in England at about the same time long remained a private association of gentlemen interested in science, the French Academicians were engaged by the King for pay to devote themselves to specific scientific problems. One of these problems of interest to us in this book were the geodetic measurements of the arcs of the meridian, intended to determine the exact dimensions of the terrestrial globe—an effort which commenced with Eratosthenes of Alexandria in the 3rd century B.C. (see p. 16) and which in the 17th century furnished essentially the size of the Earth as we know it today.

An even more important effort was, however, sponsored by the French Academy in 1670 to triangulate by telescopic methods the dimensions of the solar system; dimensions which remained almost unchanged since the days of the ancients up to that time. The correct geometrical model of the solar system was established by Johannes Kepler before 1610, but the scale of this model continued to be uncertain within very wide limits.

We mentioned before (p. 73) the dimensions attributed to this scale by Johannes Kepler or Galileo. About 1630, the Dutch astronomer G. Wendelin (1580–1660) attempted to re-determine the distance separating us from the Sun by the method of Aristarchos (see p. 22)—i.e., by measuring the extent to which the angular distance between the Sun and the Moon at quadratures (i.e., at the time of the first or last quarter) deviates from 90°. As we mentioned in the first chapter of this book, Aristarchos estimated this defect to be 3°, rendering the Sun 19.1 times as far from us as the Moon. Wendelin set out to re-determine this defect with the aid of a telescope (since telescopic observations should enable us to time the moments with much greater precision than can be done with the naked eye), and found it to be no greater than one-quarter of a degree—a value 12 times smaller than that adopted by all astronomers from Aristarchos to Kepler, and rendering the distance to the Sun 329 times as large as that separating us from the Moon. However, this value remained subject to a considerable uncertainty because of the irregular outlines of the lunar sunrise or sunset terminators, and the roughness of the Moon virtually precluded any further progress by this methods.

The only hopeful way of determining the distance of the Sun with greater accuracy seemed by the mensuration of much greater triangles in space, with vertices coinciding with the positions of the Sun, of the Earth, and another planet whose distance could be determined from parallactic displacements of its position, with respect to the star background, when observed from different places on the Earth's surface. The angles of such cosmic triangles were known at any time with ample accuracy from the theory of planetary motions. If, in addition, the length of at least one side of the triangle could be determined by using some distance on the Earth as a basis of triangulation, the dimensions of the entire triangle could be determined in absolute units.

Fig. 13. A night scene (as engraved by a contemporary artist) of the observing activity at the newly-founded Paris Observatory in the days of G. D. Cassini (around 1670), under the watchful eye of King Louis XIV (lower left). The Perrault building on the left still stands (now carrying domes on its roof) but otherwise the area is completely built up.

The French academicians of the 1670's decided, on good grounds, to identify the third vertex of their cosmic triangle with the planet Mars, which in 1672 was to approach the Earth more closely than at any time of a 16-year interval. An expedition was to be sent to Cayenne, a town in French Guiana near the equator, to measure the exact topocentric position of Mars among the stars, while their colleagues were doing the same in France. By a comparison of the positions measured simultaneously in two places separated by 7000 km, the distance to Mars could be triangulated from this baseline.

The expedition to Cayenne was apparently sanctioned by the Minister Colbert in October 1671, and passports issued to Jean Richer (?–1696) who, with the assistance of M. Meurisse, was to carry out the necessary observations. The vessel, carrying the two observers and their equipment—a merchantman of the French West India Company—departed from France at La Rochelle on

8 February 1672, on an expedition which was to last nine months and which, to quote from Fontenelle's report to the French Academy for 1673, was to 'bring all the scientific riches of the Americas to the Academy'.

Richer's arrival at French Guiana preceded the Martian opposition by a few months, and Richer—bless him—performed his tasks with skill and devotion. The story of how the change in length of the pendulum of his clock, necessary to show the correct time, led to the discovery of the oblateness of our terrestrial globe, has been told too often to need repetition in this place, and is also of only marginal interest for our main topic. But once his clock troubles were over, Richer observed the apparent positions of Mars from August through October 1672, and measured the times of the meridian transit of the planet as well as its altitude relative to the neighbouring stars; while Cassini, Picard and Roemer performed simultaneously the same observations in France.

Richer returned home safely before the end of 1672, and, to give again the word to Fontenelle, 'one expected the return of M. Richer as one expects the return of a Judge, to render verdict on the dimensions of the solar system'. This verdict was, to be sure, somewhat slow to come; for the reductions of the observations occupied the astronomers for several years, and the actual results were not published till 1684—twelve years later. But the results, and their implications, proved overwhelming. According to J. D. Cassini (1625–1712), the distance to Mars at the time of its closest approach to us in 1672 was equal to 8100 terrestrial radii or 51.6 million km; and the distance to the Sun, 21 600 radii of the Earth, or 138 million kms as against the modern value of 149.7 million km. In other words, the parallax of the Sun* was found by the French investigators to be equal to 9".5, in comparison with its modern value of 8".79.

The dimensions of the solar system were thereby for the first time established to a realistic approximation, an approximation which errs by default of less than 10 per cent of the actual value, and which was not superseded until the observations of the transits of

---

* In astronomy, the parallax of the Sun is defined as the angular semi-diameter of the Earth as seen from the respective celestial body. This angle cannot, of course, be measured directly, but is computed from a triangulated distance of the body and known dimensions of the Earth.

Venus across the Sun in 1761 and 1769 provided more favourable data for the mensuration of the solar system—and their impact on the contemporary thought was profound. For it was for the first time in history that the tremendous dimensions of the solar system, as well as the prodigious sizes of the Sun and some of the planets, were appropriately realized; and the effect of this realization was almost overpowering on educated laymen and astronomers alike. The relatively small and snug solar system of the ancients, which continued to offer a spiritual home for Galileo and Kepler, was irretrievably shattered to pieces, and with it any vestige of a claim for a preferential position in space of our Earth and its inhabitants. Instead, we found ourselves located on a tiny material speck, surrounded by seemingly endless space.

As we shall relate in subsequent chapters of this book, for centuries to come astronomers managed to surmount with their measurements and thought vastly greater cosmic distances in space than that which separates us from the Sun. But never did the realization of the emptiness of space around us administer a greater shock to human complacency and to any notion of our self-importance! It was the realization of the enormous size of the solar system and of the emptiness of space, in the last part of the 17th century, that led contemporary thinkers to echo Pascal's anguished cry: 'the eternal silence of the infinite space terrifies me'. In the years and decades to come, the isolated position of the Earth in space (which the French Encyclopaedists and Voltaire succeeded in conveying to an increasing circle of educated laymen) lost, perhaps, some of its terror. Gradually our ancestors learned to live alone in space without mental torment—and more, they developed a healthy curiosity about the extent of space outside our solar system, and separating us from the stars.

4 Distance to the Stars

In the foregoing chapter we bade farewell (by the end of the 17th century) to the story of the mensuration of the solar system—i.e., at a stage at which its structure and dimensions were known within approximately one per cent. We wish now to turn our attention to a much greater exploit of the human mind which was going on at the same time: namely, to bridge by measurement the gap separating us from the stars.

As we already explained at the beginning of our story in the first chapter, for the ancients the Earth occupied the centre of the Universe, and was surrounded by concentric heavenly spheres. To the Sun, the Moon and each one of the planets, different spheres —seven altogether—were assigned. Beyond that of the remotest planet, Saturn, was the eigth sphere of 'fixed stars'. All these spheres were supposed to be solid and incorruptible, being made of a fifth element, more refined than the base and impermanent water, earth, fire or air. Outside the sphere of the fixed stars resided the 'primum mobile'. This was the world picture of the ancients. In Christian times, the Fathers of the Church, realising the ready compatibility of this system with the Old Testament story of the Creation (a story going back to pre-Pythagorean time), adopted it for one of their own; and in the Middle Ages Dante Alighieri, by basing upon it the structure of his *Comedia Divina,* secured for it poetical immortality.

A scientific enquiry into the size of this model or the distance to the stars arose at the time of Aristarchos, with his first proposal of the heliocentric model of the solar system; for if the Earth does revolve yearly around the Sun, the apparent positions of all celestial bodies—including those of the stars—should exhibit an apparent motion, called a 'yearly parallax', as they are viewed by the ter-

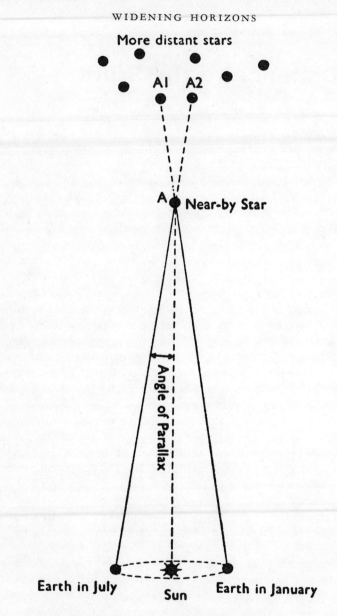

Fig. 14. The principle of the stellar parallax.

restrial observers from different vantage points in space. From the
quotation from Archimedes which we reproduced on p. 39 of this
book it is evident that both Aristarchos and he were aware of this
consequence of the heliocentric model, as well as of the fact that no
yearly parallax of the fixed stars was apparent at that time. Since,
however, the precision of absolute angular measurements attainable at that time was only of the order of 10 minutes of arc, the
absence of a yearly parallax of the stars implied that their distance
from us must be not less than $(6 \times 180°/\pi)$ or 369 times the distance
between the Earth and the Sun (a distance we usually refer to as the
'astronomical unit'), which Aristarchos thought (cf. again Chapter
1) to be equal to 360 semi-diameters of the Earth and which
Hipparchos, a century later, increased to some 1200 terrestrial
semi-diameters. In consequence, the distance to the stars on the
heliocentric systems would have to be not less than 369 astronomical units or 124,000 terrestrial semi-diameters according to
Aristarchos, or some 413,000 Earth semi-diameters according to
Hipparchos.

For many centuries following the efflorescence of the Hellenistic
civilisation, these values appeared to be so large as to create a
serious embarrassment for the protagonists of the heliocentric
system. Copernicus prudently abstained from expressing any
opinion about the distance to the stars at all. Tycho Brahe searched
assiduously (in the last quarter of the 16th century) for indications
of the yearly parallactic motion of the stars, but none larger than
one minute of arc was apparent; and its absence implied that the
distance to the stars should exceed 3700 astronomical units of 44
million terrestrial semi-diameters! The enormity of this estimate
constituted one of the principal stumbling blocks why Tycho
could not bring himself to embrace the heliocentric system. For
Galileo (who took some liberties in interpreting Tycho's observations) the fixed stars were 13 million Earth semi-diameters distant;
while Kepler said 34 million at one time, and 60 million later. But
this was decidedly too much for the surviving Ptolemaic astronomers of that age. Thus Father Christopher Clavius (1537–1612)
made out the radius of the 'sphere of fixed stars' between 20 and 45
thousand terrestrial semi-diameters in size—an estimate which
J. G. Riccioli in his *Almagestum Novum* (Bologna, 1651) increased
about five fold.

So much for the principal landmarks on the way of the gradual and century-long groping towards the barrier of 'fixed stars' enclosing the solar system. The actual distance to this elusive barrier remained out of the reach of the outstretched human mind not only throughout the entire era of pre-telescopic astronomy, but also—as we shall presently describe—long after the advent of the telescope as well. Like fata morgana in the desert, the stars continued to look at our astronomical predecessors with their enigmatic eyes from their fantastic distances, seemingly unfathomable by any measurement that could be carried out by human hand. Was it, perchance, possible to bridge this abysmal gap of space on the wings of a different kind of scientific thought?

The one which gradually emerged for consideration at about that time was based on a comparison between the Sun and the stars. With a gradual expansion of our horizons, and with the stars continuing to recede from our grasp to ever-increasing distances, astronomers have been led to realize that—unlike the planets—the stars cannot derive their light from the Sun, but must shine with light of their own. If so, are they but other Suns, only incomparably more distant?

When did it dawn upon the human mind that our Sun may be a celestial body akin to the stars, and differing from them so tremendously in brightness mainly on account of their vastly different distance? The realization that the Sun was a star should be ranked among the greatest astronomical discoveries of all times, side by side with a much earlier realization, made no doubt long before the dawn of written history, that the Sun rising in the morning is the same object which set the previous night. Moreover, as is usually the case with discoveries of this magnitude, it emerged but slowly from intuitive subconciousness over a long period of time, and cannot be ascribed to any single individual or school, or even to any country. It appears, however, that the idea was still entirely alien to the astronomy of the ancients; for no work or even allusion preserved to us from antiquity seems to contain even a germ of the suggestion that the Sun and the stars are basically one and the same thing.

For the origin of this idea we must turn to the late middle ages; but historical research is unable to locate its exact source. It seems, however, that the underlying idea was slowly gaining a foothold in the human mind not later than the 15th century. Nicholas de Cusa, Cardinal of the Roman Church, entertained in his tract *De Docta Ignorantia* (Cues, 1440) at least the germ of the ideas which, 160 years later, were to bring Giordano Bruno to the sacrificial pyre. The idea that the Sun was a star is found to have flickered briefly on the pages of the famous diaries of Leonardo da Vinci (1452–1519); but no consequences were drawn as yet from this hypothetical identity.

To a modern mind, the simplest consequence to draw would be to compare the relative brightness of the Sun and the stars, and from their observed disparity in brightness to deduce their disparity in distance. This was, however, not yet possible at that time, for the necessary link—namely, the law connecting the apparent light intensity with the distance of the source, and expressing the fact that the diminution of light intensity varies with the inverse square of the distance—was not formulated (even in a rudimentary form) until by Kepler in his *Ad Vitellionem Paralipomena*, published at Frankfurt in 1604. More than a century was yet to pass before the first effective photometer was constructed by Pierre Bouguer (1698–1758).

The first person who availed himself of this possibility to deduce a 'photometric parallax' of the stars on this basis appears to be Christiaan Huyghens (1629-1695), a great Dutch scientist contemporary with Newton. In his *Cosmotheoros* (published posthumously in 1698) Huyghens described the following experiment to determine the distance of Sirius—the brightest star of the entire sky—on the assumption that its intrinsic brightness is the same as that of our Sun. He made a tiny hole in the sealed end of a 12-foot long tube, and adjusted the effective size of this hole until the light of the Sun observed through it was equal in intensity to that of Sirius. He calculated then that the angular diameter of the hole, as seen by the observer at the other end of the 12-foot tube, was equal to one 27,664th part of the apparent diameter of the Sun. In consequence, if the Sun and Sirius are of the same intrinsic brightness, and Sirius appears so much fainter to us only because its light falls off with the square of the distance, its distance from us should clearly be equal to 27,664 times our distance from the Sun, or 27,664 astronomical units.

This is the largest figure for the distance to the stars which we have encountered in the literature up to this time, and almost ten times as large as the lower limit established by Tycho Brahe one century before. But it still represented a hopeless underestimate; as we now know, Sirius is more than 500 000 astronomical units away from us. The reasons for Huyghens's failure to come closer to the mark are, moreover, not difficult to understand. For not only is Sirius in reality intrinsically many times as bright as the Sun, but no photometric intercomparison of the two could be performed at the same time: the Sun had to be observed during the daytime, while Sirius is visible only at night, when the low prevailing light level would cause the pupil of the observer's eye to be much more distended. As a result, a photometric comparison of the Sun and of Sirius carried out by Huyghens was largely meaningless, and its outcome fortuitous.

At a later time, however, the Rev. John Michell (?–1793) following the same line of thought, arrived at a much more meaningful result, without having to perform any measurement which would have been premature in his day. He noticed that the planet Saturn around the time of its opposition appears to possess very nearly the same brightness as Vega, a northern star of approximately zero apparent magnitude. Now at the time of opposition, Saturn exhibits an apparent disc $d_\oplus = 20''$ in diameter which from the Sun would be seen at an angle of $d_\odot = 17''$. Therefore, the illuminated hemisphere of Saturn intercepts a $\sin^2 \frac{1}{4}d''_\odot$ –th or $(17\pi/720 \times 3600)^2$ –th part of light sent out by the Sun in all directions.

Now if Vega and the Sun are of equal intrinsic brightness, but Vega's apparent brightness is equal to that of Saturn, it follows (from inverse-square law for the attenuation of brightness) that it must be $720 \times 3600/17\pi$ or 48 500 times as far from the Sun as Saturn. Since, moreover, Saturn is known (from its orbital period of $29\frac{1}{2}$ years inserted in Kepler's third law) to be 9.5 times as far from the Sun as our Earth, it follows that the distance of Vega from us should amount to 461 000 astronomical units. In reading this number we can almost hold our breath, for (as we shall see later in this chapter) it represents for the first time a realistic estimate of the distance of any star—in fact, one quarter of the actual distance of Vega—obtained almost a century and a half before the trigonometric determination of Vega's distance by Struve in 1837; and the principal reason of the underestimate (which could not have been known to Michell) was the fact that—like Sirius—Vega is intrinsically much brighter than the Sun.

In the meantime, the quest for trigonometric determinations of the annual parallaxes of the stars continued unabated. There was, however, still a long and arduous way to go, for not less than three additional apparent motions of the stars had to be discovered and identified before their annual parallaxes could be at last identified. All three of these are connected with motions in which our Earth takes part, but while the first two—nutation and aberration—are due exclusively to the motion of our own terrestrial observing platform, the third—the so-called proper motions of the stars—are compounded by the combined effect of the Earth's translational motion with the Sun through space, together with similar motions of other stars with respect to us.

To take up first the nutation, it had been pointed out already by Stevin in 1605 that the double motion (i.e., axial rotation and annual revolution) ascribed to the Earth by Copernicus does not really exhaust fully the case. For the 'precession of the equinoxes' —the effect of which were noted already by Hipparchos in the 2nd century B.C.—reveals the existence of a conical motion of the terrestrial axis of rotation in space akin to that of a spinning top. Since, however, this third motion of the Earth turns out to be very slow (one complete revolution of our terrestrial 'spinning top' takes some 25,800 years) it did not unduly excite the theologians, and was completely forgotten in the decree of the Roman Inquisition of 1632 which attempted otherwise to restrict severely the Earth's freedom of motion on the grounds of biblical exegesis.

With the advent of the Newtonian mechanics at the end of the 17th century, the cause of the precession of the equinoxes was identified with the luni-solar attraction on the equatorial bulge of the Earth (due to the rotation of our planet). But there is more to this action, for not only does the terrestrial axis of rotation, inclined by $23° 27'$ to the plane of its orbit (i.e., the 'ecliptic')— complete one revolution around a direction perpendicular to the ecliptic every 25,800 years, but it wobbles about its mean position in a much shorter period. This effect—the so-called 'nutation'— constitutes the periodic part of the motion of the Earth about its centre of gravity in the external field of force. To an observer unaware of it, the positions of the stars in the equatorial system of co-ordinates would seem to exhibit a spurious apparent motion tracing the movement of the terrestrial pole on the celestial sphere.

The principal effects of nutation were discovered by the British astronomer James Bradley (1693–1762), since 1721 a professor of astronomy at Oxford and later the third Astronomer Royal—the greatest of the holders of that office—and a veritable 'vir incomparabilis', as he was called more than a century later by his peer Bessel. On the basis of observations extending over more than 20 years, Bradley identified in 1748 the principal term of nutation, giving rise to fluctuations of stellar positions with an amplitude of $9''.22$ in a period 18.61 years of the revolution of the line of the nodes of the lunar orbit. The principal amount of nutation is, therefore, due to the disturbing effects of lunar attraction; but that of the Sun contributes an additional term oscillating semi-annually with an amplitude of $0''.55$.

But this was not the only, or even the largest, contribution of Bradley to the study of apparent positions of the stars. In 1725, from careful observations of γ Draconis (a star passing nearly through the zenith of Bradley's observing site then at Kew, near London), Bradley detected the existence of another annual displacement of its position in the course of which the star describes an apparent ellipse in the sky with a semi-major axis of $20''.47$, and a semi-minor axis equal to $20''.47 \sin \beta$, where β denotes the star's latitude in ecliptical (rather than equatorial) co-ordinates. At the pole of the ecliptic ($\beta = 90°$), this apparent motion becomes, therefore, circular; but reduces to a rectilinear oscillation in its plane.

As to the cause of this oscillation, Bradley himself identified it correctly with the effects of the annual revolution of the Earth around the Sun, and due to the fact that the velocity v of the Earth in this orbit bears a finite ratio to the velocity c with which light propagates through space. A vectorial sum of these two kinds of motion—i.e., of light relative to a moving observer—leads us to expect that the ratio $v/c = \tan 20''.47$; which for $c = 299,776$ km/sec leads to $v = 29.75$ as the (mean) velocity with which the Earth revolves around the Sun. As, moreover, we know that the Earth completes this revolution in one year of $31,558,150$ seconds, the mean distance of the Earth (i.e., our 'astronomical unit') as determined from the aberration effect would come out to be $149,500,000$ km, as compared with its modern value of $149,597,890$ km determined by radar. Bradley could not, to be sure, ascertain the value of the aberration effect as accurately as we know it now, nor did he know so well the speed of light. Even so, however, he could determine in 1725 from his measurements, coupled with Roemer's determination of the velocity of light, the distance to the Sun almost as accurately as was done by the French observers of the Martian opposition in 1673.

Modern astronomy owes much indeed to these discoveries of Bradley—discoveries which earned him a rightful place in the history of science side by side with Hipparchos, Tycho Brahe or Bessel. For as long as the measured positions of the stars could deviate from each other by as much as 30″ through the combined effects of nutation and aberration, it was a hopeless task to obtain consistency among them necessary to measure a stellar parallax which could amount to less than 1″. It was only after the observations were corrected for the predictable periodic effects of nutation and aberration that serious effort could be justified to suppress the observational and instrumental errors to levels at which the quest for parallactic motions of the stars could stand a real chance of success. Before, however, this could become true, another discovery was yet waiting behind the scene, whose entry was necessary to complete the stage: and that was the realization that, quite apart from the motion of the Earth, the stars exhibit also proper motions of their own.

A discovery of the proper motions of the stars antedated, in fact (although narrowly) Bradley's discovery of the phenomenon of aberration, and was due to his predecessor in the office of British Astronomer Royal. Early in 1718, Edmond Halley (of whom we have already heard in the preceding chapter) communicated to the Royal Society of London a paper entitled 'Considerations on the Change of the Latitudes of Some of the Principal Fixt Stars', in which he compared the contemporary positions of some stars with those contained in Ptolemy's *Almagest* (2nd century A.D.) and wrote: 'I was surprized to find the Latitudes of three of the principal Stars of Heaven directly to contradict the supposed greater Obliquity of the Ecliptick, which seems confirmed by the Latitudes of most of the rest, they being set down in the old Catalogue as though the Plain of the Earths Orb(it) had changed its situation, among the fixt Stars, about 20′ since the time of Hipparchus. . . . Yet the three Stars Palilicium or the Bulls Eye, Sirius and Arcturus do contradict this rule directly. . . . What shall we say then? It is scarce credible that the Antients could be deceived in so plain a matter, three Observers confirming each other. Again these Stars being the most conspicuous in Heaven, are in all probability nearest to the Earth, and if they have any particular Motion of their own, it is most likely to be perceived in them, which in so long a time as 1800 Years may shew itself by the alteration of their places, though it be utterly imperceptible in the space of a single Century of Years . . . This Argument seems not unworthy of the Royal Society's Consideration, to whom I humbly offer the plain Fact as I find it, and would be glad to have their opinion.'

What Halley referred to rather obliquely in the preceding quotation was the fact that, since ancient times, the three stars, Palilicium, Sirius and Arcturus, have changed their apparent position in the sky by amounts exceeding the probable errors of the measurements, thus disclosing the existence of secular proper motions of these (and possibly other stars) unrelated to any kind of motions of the Earth within the solar system. The modern values of the proper motions of Sirius and Arcturus in the sky are known to be $1''.32$ and $2''.28$ per annum. On the other hand, the ancient positions collected in the *Almagest* were really measured by Hipparchos in the 2nd century B.C.—i.e., some 1800 years before the time of Halley. During this interval, therefore, the two stars mentioned above had had time to displace their positions in the sky by $40'$ and $68'$ respectively, i.e., values larger than the apparent angular diameter of the Sun or the Moon.

The establishment of such motions destroyed for ever in the human mind the notion that the position of the stars were 'fixed' in the sky, and that term could hereafter be applied to them only for the sake of picturesqueness. Actually these stars—all the stars around us, in fact—are in perpetual motion, and their positions appear to be fixed only if we consider them over ephemeral time intervals, comparable with those of human lives. However, several stars (such as Sirius, α Centauri, or Procyon, for instance) are known to exhibit proper motions exceeding $1''$ per annum, and their annual parallax would manifest itself only as a periodic wiggle on their otherwise rectilinear motion across the sky.

The quest for such indications of parallactic motion continued after Bradley's time without letup, and long without any success. In the last quarter of the 18th century, William Herschel (of whom much more will be said in the next chapter) tried repeatedly to detect the parallax of the stars by searching for differential displacements in close pairs of stars of very different brightness. Since the brighter components of such pairs were supposed to be much nearer to us than their faint companions (and thus exhibit a proportionally larger parallax), Herschel pressed his search for their differential parallactic displacements with great assiduity. Yet years went by, and no annual parallax ever transpired from their motion. Instead, Herschel discovered something else: namely, indications of orbital motion around their common centre of gravity. Many of Herschel's close pairs proved to be, not mere 'optical' combinations of two stars at different distance accidentally seen in the same direction of the sky, but genuine physical systems of two stars moving under the influence of their mutual attraction. The existence of a new class of stellar systems has thus been detected in this way—but still no parallax!

However, the hand on the cosmic clock measuring human achievements was already approaching the time when the age-long quest for stellar parallax was finally to be crowned with success. The time when this clock struck was in the year 1837; and, as it sometimes happens in the annals of science, it was not one, but three stars which revealed their distance to us at almost the same time: namely, α Centauri, α Lyrae (Wega)—two of the brightest stars in the entire sky—and, in addition, a little inconspicuous northern double star called 61 Cygni.

The story of how it happened deserves to be given in more than a few words. The three heroes of this episode in the history of astronomy were Friedrich Wilhelm Bessel (1784–1846) of Königsberg, Thomas Henderson (1798–1844) at that time Her Majesty's Astronomer at the Cape of Good Hope, and Friedrich Georg Wilhelm Struve (1793–1864) the first astronomer of that distinguished family, then working at the Dorpat Observatory in Russia. Henderson chose α Centauri, and Struve Vega, for their measurements on account of their outstanding apparent brightness, which to them suggested proximity; while Bessel selected 61 Cygni because of its large proper motion (5.″20 per annum). Henderson's observations, which eventually led to his result, commenced on the Cape in April 1831, while Struve began his work on Vega in 1835, and Bessel in 1837. All three observers had different instruments at their disposal: Henderson, a mural quadrant (perhaps the least suitable of the three); Struve, a 9-inch refractor equipped with a filar micrometer; while Bessel utilized a $6\frac{1}{4}$-inch heliometer with its split-beam technique—a type of instrument which remained unrivalled for angular measurements of highest precision until the advent of photography.

The first results to be published were those of Struve, who in his *Mensurae Micrometricae* (1837) recorded that . . . 'As for the parallax (of Vega), we have found $\pi = 0''.125$ with a probable error of $0''.055$. We can therefore conclude that the parallax is very small, as it probably lies between $0''.07$ and $0''.08$. But, indeed, we cannot give it yet absolutely'. This result was known to Bessel when he commenced his own observations of 61 Cygni in 1838; but before the end of that year he was able to announce the parallax of this star to be equal to $0''.314 \pm 0''.014$ (p.e.). As for Henderson, although he was the first one to commence observations of α Centauri which resulted in the determination of its distance, difficulties of overseas communications before the days of steamships, caused publication delays—with the result that he was the last one to publish his parallax of $0''.76$ (the latter did not appear in print till 1838). Thus while Struve was the first one to publish the results of his work in 1837, the first reliable parallax of a star (61 Cygni) was published in 1838, and actually obtained by Bessel that year; but the nearest of the three stars proved to be α Centauri selected by Henderson.

The important thing is, to be sure, not so much which parallax was determined or published first, but which parallax actually dispelled all doubts of the contemporary astronomers that the long-searched-for effect had finally been found. And there can be no doubt that it was the parallax of 61 Cygni, and not that of α Lyrae (or α Centauri) which actually provided this assurance; for it had a probable error of only $\pm 0''.014$ to be applied to a parallax of $0''.314$ (its best modern value being $0''.299 \pm 0''.003$). The deep impression which this memorable achievement created in astronomical circles is reflected in the following piece of sonorous Victorian prose, taken from an address by Sir John Herschel (son of William Herschel, the principal hero of our next chapter) on the occasion

Fig. 15.   **FRIEDRICH WILHELM BESSEL**
(1784–1846)

He fathomed the distance to the stars.

of the award of a Gold Medal by the Royal Astronomical Society of London to Bessel in 1841:

'I congratulate you, and myself, that we have lived to see the great and hitherto impassable barrier to our excursions into the sidereal Universe—that barrier against which we chafed so long and so vainly—almost simultaneously overleaped at three different points. It is the greatest and most glorious triumph which practical astronomy has ever witnessed. Perhaps I ought not to speak so strongly—perhaps I should hold some reserve in favour of the bare possibility that it may be all an illusion and that further researchers, as they have repeatedly before, so may now fail to substantiate this noble result. But I confess myself unequal to such prudence under such excitement. Let us rather accept the joyful omens of the time and trust that, as the barrier has begun to yield, it will speedily be prostrated. Such results are among the fairest flowers of human civilization'.

And well may we join Sir John in the spirit of his eulogy, for his enthusiasm was not ill-placed, nor did the results on which he reported prove illusory. For the barrier to the stars has indeed been crossed. The parallax $\pi = 0''.314$ for 61 Cygni or 0.125 for Vega would mean that, at their distance, the radius of the terrestrial orbit around the Sun would be seen under this angle or, in other words, their distance proves to be 206 265 π^{-1} Astronomical Units— 619,000 A.U. for 61 Cygni, or 1,650,000 A.U. for Vega. These numbers are too large to be used extensively in practice. Therefore, astronomers have adopted another unit of length to measure the distance to the stars: namely, one parsec, at which one astronomical unit would appear to have an angular diameter of one second of arc (i.e., to have a parallax $\pi = 1''$). In other words, the distance of one parsec should be equal to 206 265 astronomical units.

Expressed in terms of this unit, 61 Cygni is 3.3 parsecs away from us; and Vega, 8 parsecs; while α Centauri—the nearest of the three and the nearest star to us in space—is at a distance of a mere 1.32 parsecs. Light, the fastest messenger in the Universe, travelling at a velocity of a little less than 300 000 km/sec, would need to spend 3.26 years to traverse the distance of one parsec. Therefore 61 Cygni is 10.9 light years away from us; Vega, 26 light years; and α Centauri, 4.3 light years. Compare these times with 499 seconds or 8 min 19 sec which light takes to traverse the distance separating us from the Sun, a little over an hour to reach Saturn—the farther-most planet known to the ancients; or some 4 hours which sunlight takes to reach Pluto—the outermost sentinel of our solar system. A disparity between 4 hours and 4 years in time indicates the gap of no-man's land separating our solar system from the nearest stars. Nevertheless, between 1837 and 1839 this gap was at last bridged by astronomical triangulation using the dimensions of the terrestrial orbit around the Sun as a baseline; and the continuation of this story would belong to a more technical treatise on astronomy. In what follows, we shall take leave of this subject at this juncture, and turn our attention to greater vistas which commenced to open up to the astronomer's gaze around that time.

5 The Space Widens

After having traced the age-long quest for a determination of the distance of the stars to its triumphant first success in the last chapter, let us turn back to follow the other exploits of observational astronomy since the discovery of the telescope. The road to further development of the astronomical telescope itself in post-Galilean days was rather circuitous and, in retrospect, replete with misunderstandings. In the years following the generation of Galileo, the principal obstacle to increased telescopic power was seen in the chromatic aberration of the objective, which increases with the curvature of its optical surface. The easiest way to lessen it seemed to be to diminish this curvature, and increase the focal length of the lens.

As a result, the telescopes began to grow inordinately in length, to usher in the first geological age of optical Dinosaurs characterized by small heads and huge bodies. The aperture of their objectives seldom exceeded 6–8 inches; but their focal ratios became extremely large, leading to focal lengths in excess of those of most telescopes existing at the present time. For example, the telescope with which Johannes Hevelius (see Figure 12) carried out at Danzig most of his observations of the lunar surface had a focal length of 49 metres! Needless to say, instruments of such length could be but crudely mounted. Astronomers of the second half of the 17th century had mostly to dispense with any kind of tubes, and the objective was mounted at the end of a long pole directed to different parts of the sky by means of ropes and pulleys.

Sometimes, in desperation, astronomers dispensed with the mounting altogether, fixed their objectives to the roof of a building, and waited on the ground for a transit of the celestial object literally with an eyepiece in their hand. No wonder that, under such circumstances, Hevelius preferred the unaided eye for the measurements of stellar positions, until the end of his life. This was the truly heroic age of observational astronomy—the age of Hevelius, Huyghens or the Cassinis; and their discoveries—rings and satellites of Saturn, motion and maps of the Moon, etc.—are not seen in proper perspective until one considers the crude telescopic means at their disposal.

In the end, the long-necked telescopic Dinosauri of the second half of the 17th century vanished from the scene under their own weight as much as under the impact of new developments in astronomical optics which had taken place in the meantime: namely, a gradual introduction into practical use of the astronomical reflector. The idea underlying such an instrument was known to Galileo Galilei (and described by him, through the mouth of Sagredo, in his *Dialogues on the Two Great World Systems*); but it was not translated into actual practice until in 1671 by Isaac Newton. Besides this positive contribution Newton left, however, our science also a negative legacy in the form of a mistaken assertion that it was impossible to achromatize a convex lens. The incorrectness of this assertion was, to be sure, proved in 1733 by Chester More Hall, and the first achromatic objective was actually produced by John Dollond around 1759. Such was, however, the weight of any opinion expressed by Newton (as well as the technical difficulties in producing achromatic objectives of larger size) throughout the 18th century that the pendulum continued to swing from dioptic to catoptric systems, and the stage thus set for the first period of efflorescence of the astronomical reflector at the hands of William Herschel (1738–1822).

The history of this one-time musician and organist, who relatively late in life turned to astronomy to transform completely our view of the Universe, belongs among the most enchanting stories encountered in the entire history of astronomy, and in following it we shall find ourselves once more entering the rapids from which we shall emerge to a virtually new world. The hero of this particular episode of our science will be no sleepwalker like Johannes Kepler or shrewd stargazer like Galileo Galilei, but a personality no less interesting than our two founding fathers from the beginning of the 17th century.

William Herschel, the discoverer and founder of stellar astronomy, was born on 15 November 1738 in Hanover, as one out of ten children born to Isaac Herschel, musician and oboist in the Royal Hanoverian Foot Guards, and his wife Anna Ilse Moritzen of Neustadt. By that time the Herschel family had not been settled in Hanover for long, for he descended from the Protestants who were driven out of Bohemia, on account of their Reformed Faith, during the Thirty Years' War about a century before. When the Kingdom of Bohemia came under a Catholic Ruler and, under the Edict of 1627, all Protestants were banished from its frontiers, among those who preferred exile to giving up the faith of his fathers was one Hans Herschel—a brewer by trade—and great-grandfather of our astronomer.

Like many families which fled from Bohemia under similar circumstances, the Herschels settled first on the Saxon side of the Bohemian frontier near Dresden (in villages still bearing Czech names) in the hope of an eventual return; and Hans's son Abraham —grandfather of our astronomer—was born there in exile in 1651. (The predominance of biblical names was common among the Protestants of that age). In time he became a gardener by trade, but is reported to have been very fond of arithmetic and drawing, as well as of music. Isaac, his fourth and last child, was born in 1707 in Hohensatz. The years went by, however, and the family which had despaired of a return to their old homeland, moved to Hanover in 1731, where a year later Isaac Herschel got married. Of the ten children who were born to him, two will concern our narrative: Friedrich Wilhelm—the future great astronomer—was the third son, and his sister Caroline Lucretia—his future indefatigable assistant and astronomer in her own right—was born on 16 March 1750.

All the children inherited the musical talent of their father, who appears to have been a man remarkably cultivated for his age; but even otherwise their schooling was not neglected. Caroline Herschel preserved for us her recollection of the evening family talks, when she lay awake listening to her father and brothers debating on scientific subjects: 'My brother William', she wrote, 'and his Father were often arguing with such warmth that my Mother's interference became necessary when the names of Leibnitz, Newton and Euler sounded rather too loud for the repose of her little ones, who ought to be in school by seven in the morning. But it seemed that to the brothers retiring to their room, where they shared the same bed, my brother William had still a great deal to say; and frequently it happened that when he stopped for an assent or a reply, he found that his hearers had gone to sleep.' William's interest in astronomy was, therefore, certainly planted early in his life. But it was to be an avocation; for in order to earn a living he was to follow in his father's footsteps, and joined the band of the Hanoverian Guards as an oboist at the age of fourteen.

It is almost impossible to trace the fortunes of William Herschel or the other members of his family for several years, on account of the general turmoil in Europe during the years of his youth, to which army people were particularly exposed. It appears, however, that in April 1756 the movement of his regiment brought him for the first time to England, which was later to become his second home. It is certain that he returned there in 1759—no longer in military service—to seek his livelihood as a musician, and during the next 23 years of his life in England his principal pursuit was music. In this pursuit we find him in 1759 at Durham to conduct Lord Darlington's band; between 1762–66 he directed public concerts at Leeds; but in 1766 he became the organist at Halifax, and in 1767 he came to Bath as concert director and organist in the fashionable Octagon Chapel. This was already a position of some distinction—socially as well as professionally—and Herschel was gradually joined there by other members of his family; in particular, his sister Caroline came over in August 1772.

Throughout the most part of his life, William Herschel kept a diary in which he recorded faithfully many events of his life, and which proves a valuable source for the history of our subject. A year after Caroline joined him, immediately after an interesting entry that . . . 'I paid £15 10s. 0d. for a handsome suit of clothes, it being then the fashion for gentlemen to be very genteely dressed', there occurs a note, on 10 May 1773, 'Bought a book on astronomy, and one of astronomical tables'—a memorable note in the history of science, for Herschel's career as one of the greatest astronomical observers can be dated to that time. Which book it was we find recorded in another place of the diary where we read . . . 'In the spring of the year 1773 I began to provide myself with the materials for Astronomical purposes. The 19th April I bought a Hadley's quadrant, and soon after Ferguson's *Astronomy*'.

It has sometimes been claimed for Ferguson, on the strength of this evidence, that it was his book which attracted William Herschel to astronomy. Although Caroline's childhood recollections disclose that it may not have provided the first inspiration, it without doubt rekindled interests dormant in his mind; and this may be the most important contribution which Ferguson made to our science. James Ferguson (1710–1776) was himself a rather interesting personality. He began his life as a poor shepherd lad, watching the stars go by as he lay on his back in the heather of his native Scottish highlands; and although he never acquired much professional knowledge or made any discoveries, he enjoyed a well-deserved reputation in his time as a popularizer.

Ferguson's *Astronomy* (1769) is now a book long forgotten by the public; but to the historian of science in England it still offers an interesting mirror of its times. Of its 22 chapters, all but one were devoted to the solar system, and only one (the last) to the fixed stars —a division which reflected the contemporary attitude towards the celestial phenomena. For these was still very little known about the stars at that time beyond their positions in the sky and the fact that, being at an enormous distance from the Sun, they must have a light of their own. A very slight proper motion of half a dozen stars had been detected by Halley and astronomers of subsequent generations, who also discovered a few first variable stars in the sky. Nevertheless, the number of stars in the Flamsteed *Catalogue* of that time did not exceed 3000, and Ferguson considered that the number of stars . . . 'is much less than is generally imagined'.

A few other quotations from Ferguson's *Astronomy*, concerning subjects to which Herschel was later to give so much attention, will confirm the vague ideas still current at that time about the nature of the heavenly bodies outside the confines of the solar system:

'There is a remarkable tract around the Heavens called the Milky Way from its peculiar whiteness, which was formerly thought to be owing to a vast number of very small stars therein; but the telescope shows it to be quite otherwise; and, therefore, its whiteness must be owing to some other cause.'

'There are several whitish spots in the Heavens, which appear magnified and more luminous when seen through a telescope; yet without any stars in them. One of these is in Andromeda's girdle.'

'Cloudy stars are so called from their misty appearance. They look like dim stars to the naked eye; but through a telescope they appear broad illuminated parts of the sky; in some of which is one star, in others more. Five of these are mentioned by Ptolemy . . . The most remarkable of all the cloudy stars is that in the middle of Orion's sword. It looks like a gap in the sky, through which one may see (as it were) part of a much brighter region',

The idea of light shining through rifts in a dark curtain echoes the ancient conception of the Universe as a system of concentric spheres, the outer and highest of all being heavenly light. For in spite of Galileo or Kepler, the cobwebs of the Ptolemaic cosmology still hung about the minds of many astronomers. It was reserved for Herschel to brush them all finally away.

At the time when a perusal of Ferguson's *Astronomy* awakened Herschel's interest in the subject, the 35-year old musician had no inkling of the full magnitude of the revolution in astronomy which he was about to initiate. At first he was merely eager to verify with his own eyes the existence of the celestial phenomena described by Ferguson and others. To this end Herschel borrowed from a local optician a $2\frac{1}{2}$ foot long reflecting telescope magnifying about 40 times, but it did not satisfy him for long. Having learned that a larger telescope would have to be custom-made—at a price which he found prohibitive—Herschel resorted to self help, and (unknown to him as yet) his do-it-yourself telescopes soon exceeded in performance not only all other commercial products, but also such telescopes as were in the hands of all professional astronomers of his time.

For several years he thus carried on alone—a musician of increasing reputation in the daytime, but at night laying down the foundation for more momentous accomplishments. As for many amateur astronomers who embarked on their avocation under similar circumstances, the first observatory of William Herschel was the street of the town where he lived. Fortunately, public illumination in Bath at that time still left much to be desired by the pedestrian, and its streets were almost as dark at night as in the country. One night in December 1779, as Herschel was observing the Moon with a 7-foot telescope stationed in front of his house, a gentleman passing by stopped to look at the instrument, and when Herschel took his eye off the telescope, he asked if he might be permitted to look in. Next morning he called at Herschel's house to thank him for his civility and introduced himself: he was Dr. Thomas Watson, a well-connected fashionable physician and amateur scientist who happened also to be a Fellow of the Royal Society in London. He readily undertook to introduce Herschel to his friends and, through them, to the British astronomical 'establishment' of that time. In this way, the road was paved for Herschel to embark on his scientific career—and to immortality.

Herschel soon found his initial telescope quite inadequate to satisfy his expectation, and clearly saw that no real progress in astronomy beyond the level reflected in Ferguson's book was possible without a new systematic survey of the entire sky. This the 35-year old musician set before himself as the task to which he would devote the rest of his life, and, when he departed from this world on 25 August 1822 almost fifty years later, he left behind him our astronomical science and our outlook on the Universe changed almost beyond recognition—largely due to his own efforts.

Once Herschel made up his mind to this undertaking, the first step he had to take was to equip himself with more adequate optical instruments for his observations. Since, as we have already mentioned, these could not be ordered from any manufacturer, he had perforce to become his own optician in the daytime before he could observe with his tools at night. That, in this effort, he turned to develop the astronomical reflector was obvious; for discs of speculum metal could be cast with much greater ease than blocks of glass of comparable size; and the polishing into shape of a concave mirror represented a simpler task than the grinding of a lens—and one at which Herschel became singularly adept in a very few years. In fact, so adept did he soon become at it that when it was no longer possible for him to follow the double career of a musician and an astronomer and when, in 1782, he gave up music for good, he became for a time almost a professional instrument-maker, augmenting by their sale his rather meagre stipend as King's Astronomer given to him by George III, until a late marriage to a wealthy widow and heiress in 1788 made it no longer necessary to make ends meet from his own earnings.

Altogether William Herschel is known to have made about 70 telescopes for sale, which earned him over £14 000—no small sum in those days—but those best known were made famous by his own work. The first of them was his 7-foot telescope (he made several of this size) of 6-inch aperture, with which Herschel discovered in 1781 the new planet Uranus, thus extending the size of the solar system beyond the confines known to the ancients. His chef d'oeuvre was the famous 20-foot telescope of 18.7-inch free aperture (f/13.3) completed in 1782. It was mainly with the aid of this excellent instrument that Herschel 'coelorum perrupit claustra', and opened to us for the first time the vistas of a much vaster world.

His subsequent 40-foot reflector (of 48-inch aperture) completed in 1789, was of the nature of a tour-de-force, and never proved a success in the technical sense of the word; for a maintenance of the true optical form of its metallic mirror in all positions, or the mounting and control of so large an instrument, confronted Herschel with problems which were still insuperable in his time. Yet, in spite of these limitations, he was the first astronomer in history to use with effect the telescopic magnifying powers in excess of 1000; and the optical quality of his mirrors was such as to show stars 'round as a button', to the astonishment of his contemporaries.

A historian of science will find no less astonishing the breadth of Herschel's interest as an observer, which left out virtually nothing that could be seen in the sky. The solar system he enriched by his discovery of a new planet (Uranus, 1781), of the polar caps on Mars and a remarkably close determination of the length of its day; of the first two satellites (Ariel and Umbriel) of Uranus (1787) discovered with the 20-foot telescope, and of two new satellites of Saturn (Mimas and Enceladus), the first discovery made with the giant 40-foot telescope in 1789.

The main object of Herschel's scientific curiosity and of the majority of his published investigations was, however, the realm of the stars. His greatest enterprise proved to be a systematic survey of the northern heavens (extended later by his son John to the southern hemisphere), to which he was to devote most of his observational time between 1780–1811, and on which he employed all his telescopes in turn. In the course of this work—the first great effort to this end—he discovered and catalogued some 2500 nebulae or star clusters, and over 800 double stars. For the multitude of single ordinary stars he instituted his famous 'star gauges'—i.e., counts of the number of stars visible through a given telescope in

Fig. 16. The 20-foot telescope of William Herschel (1782).

different parts of the sky. Moreover, this was not only a collection of data on a grand scale; for with Herschel theory and observation went hand in hand, and whatever he did was part of a definite plan to throw light on the structure of the stellar universe around us.

Herschel was, therefore, not only the founder of stellar astronomy in general, but he became also a pioneer of statistical astronomy, both as regards the collection and interpretation of the data. Two problems in particular originated with him. One was the investigation of the form of the stellar system which we inhabit, and of its relation to the stellar systems around us; the other was the determination of the Sun's motion among the neighbouring stars.

Let us say a few words on this latter subject first. As we mentioned already in the last chapter, the ancient conception of the heavens as the firmament of fixed stars was shattered at the beginning of the 18th century, when Edmond Halley pointed out that several of the conspicuous stars in the sky had displaced their positions since ancient times by angles equal to two or three apparent diameters of the Sun or the Moon, and that, therefore, the stars possess proper motions of their own. During the years which elapsed since Halley's discovery to the time of William Herschel,

Fig. 16a. The 40-foot telescope of William Herschel (1789).

other observers (Lambert, Mayer, Maskelyne) noted several other instances of this kind, so that more than 40 stars were known to exhibit proper motion by the time when Herschel turned to this problem in 1783. Herschel realised that such proper motions are the resultants of two different components: namely, of true proper motions ('peculiar motions') of the stars through space, and a 'parallactic' (i.e., apparent) motion due to the fact that our Sun with all its planets is moving through space as well, so that the positions of other stars are observed by us from a 'moving platform'.

How to separate the two? Herschel realized in 1783 that if the directions of the peculiar motions were distributed in space at random, the parallactic component could be isolated by taking the average of total motions observed in different directions of the sky. In other words, the direction of the solar motion through space could be found out by observing in which part of the sky the stars are apparently receding from each other in front of us, and converging behind us—like sparks from the chimney of a moving steam locomotive—and from the rate of their dispersal in front of us, and convergence behind us, the velocity of our motion through space could be deduced.

William Herschel was the first astronomer to develop this argument—which all subsequent investigations could improve only in detail—and put it to task. If we consider, moreover, the relative scarcity of the data at his disposal, we must own that he did remarkably well; for already in 1786 he placed the point to which we are heading in space (i.e., the position of the so-called 'apex' of the solar motion) near the star λ Herculis in the sky, only a few degrees from the place where we believe it to be today. As to the absolute velocity of this motion, Herschel could not determine it without ambiguity, as he did not know yet the distance to the stars. Instead, he expressed it in terms of the unknown distance to Sirius. He guessed, however, the latter with some luck—having made it equal to 6 years and $4\frac{1}{2}$ months of light time (the modern value being $8\frac{1}{2}$ light years)—and, on this basis, deduced the Sun to move through space at 14 km/sec (against the modern value of 20 km/sec)—not a bad value for the first estimate!

In this way, William Herschel added one more motion to the Earth—sharing the translation motion of the entire solar system through space, with a speed equal to approximately two-thirds of its orbital velocity around the Sun. Accordingly, the true trajectory of the Earth in space is not a mildly eccentric plane ellipse, but rather a three-dimensional spiral along which we are dragged through space by the Sun. Its determination was bound to add to the theological complexities of accounting for our position in space; but by that time the theologians were about to remove Copernicus and Galileo from the list of prohibited books—this actually happened in 1822, just about one month before Herschel's death—and gave up any serious attempts to regulate the motions of the celestial bodies by the word of the Bible. The blasphemous remark of Laplace to Napoleon (who noted the absence of any reference to God in the latter's *Mécanique Céleste*) that he 'had no need of such a hypothesis' belongs to the same time.

As to Great Britain where Herschel resided, all leading astronomical positions at that time were still occupied by theologians—the Astronomer Royal, the Rev. N. Maskelyne, the Rev. Th. Hornsby, Savilian Professor of Astronomy at Oxford, as well as Alexander Wilson, Professor of the same subject at Edinburgh, were all doctors of divinity (Wilson also of medicine), and had to pay at least lip-service to the views held by their bishops. When another English divine, the Rev. John Michell, put forward a view in 1767 which, to us, demonstrated conclusively the existence of physical double stars in the sky, he felt constrained to explain this was due . . . 'to whatever cause this may be owing, whether to their mutual gravitation, or to some other law or appointment of the Creator'. There is, however, no evidence that Herschel, like Kepler before him, ran into any ecclesiastical opposition during his life, and remained on terms of personal friendship with all three official astronomers of his time throughout their lives *.

But let us now return to the second, and greater, problem which became the central motive of Herschel's scientific life: namely, that of the structure of the heavens, and the size of the universe which we inhabit. Does it consist of an immense number of solar systems

---

* The Rev. Dr. Hornsby appeared to be a bit stand-offish towards William Herschel at the beginning of his career, but not so the Rev. Dr. Maskelyne. The latter visited Herschel in 1777 at Bath; 'but'—as Caroline Herschel remarked in her diary—'not being introduced as Astronomer Royal, my Brother only pronounced him (after having had several hours' spirited conversation with him) to be 'a devil of a fellow'—after he had seen him to the door.'

similar to our own? Such questions had arisen, to be sure, in the minds of astronomers repeatedly before Herschel's time. Thus Thomas Wright (1711–1786) in his *New Hypothesis of the Universe* (1750) had already considered that what we see as the Milky Way girdling the sky was, in effect, the projection of a gigantic stellar system of stars extending farthest out in the plane of the luminous belt. Immanuel Kant (1724–1804) the famous philosopher of Königsberg, adopted this view in his *Theorie des Himmels* (1755). In 1761, Johann Heinrich Lambert (1728–1777) in his *Cosmologische Briefe* (1761) elaborated again a theory of the hierarchy of stellar systems, of which that of the Milky Way was only one unit. There might be an even larger number of such Milky Ways in space, forming a still higher system. All these opinions constituted, however, philosophical speculations of the kind in which Democritos indulged in the 4th century B.C., and, as such, were only bubbles of pure thought which Herschel was the first to confront with actual observations.

In the first of his two papers 'On the Construction of the Heavens,' published in 1784 and 1785, Herschel (echoing Galileo) stated that 'On applying the telescope to a part of the *via lactea* I found that it completely resolved the whole whitish appearance into small stars... The glorious multitude of stars of all possible sizes that presented themselves to my view was truly astonishing; but as the dazzling brighness of glittering stars may easily mislead us so far as to estimate their number greater than it really is, I endeavoured to ascertain this point by counting many fields and computing, from a mean of them, what a certain portion of the Milky Way may contain'. Hence, a study of the structure of the Milky Way could be reduced to star counts. Assuming, moreover, that stars are of the same intrinsic brightness and equally scattered through space, we could deduce from the numbers of stars of given apparent brightness counted in the telescopic field of view the extent of our stellar system in space.

Herschel made more than 3000 of such sample counts in different directions and through different telescopes from the 1770's up to the early years of the next century. Their results disclosed that the system of our Milky Way forms a disc-shaped agglomeration, extending over 800 times the distance between the Sun and Sirius in the plane of the Milky Way, but only 150 times in the direction perpendicular to it, containing altogether some hundred million individual stars. Since the distance to Sirius is now known to be about $8\frac{1}{2}$ light years, the dimensions of the Milky Way system would, according to Herschel, amount to some 7000 light years in the equatorial plane, and some 1300 light years in a plane perpendicular to it.

These were Herschel's views in the last decade of the 18th century. By 1806, when he could better estimate the apparent brightness of the stars by inter-comparison of their images as seen through the telescopes of different apertures, he increased the dimensions of the Galaxy to 2300 Sirius-distances (i.e., 20 000 light years) in the plane of the Milky Way, and 500 Sirius-distances (4000 light years) in the direction of the galactic pole, and in 1818 — at the age of eighty — he termed the dimensions of the Milky Way 'fathomless'. Yet these dimensions, huge as they appeared to be to Herschel's contemporaries, are still about as much underestimated as Kepler underestimated the size of the solar system. And we can scarcely blame Herschel for not having done any better, for the final dimensions of our galactic system were not properly settled until 1952 by Baade.

In estimating the dimensions of our Milky Way system, Herschel assumed, to simplify the argument, that all stars he counted in the field of view of his telescopes were of equal intrinsic brightness, so that differences in their apparent brightness were due solely to their different distance. That this was not so in reality was established by Herschel himself — by his discovery of physical binaries in the sky, consisting of two stars in close proximity to each other (since they revolve around a common centre of gravity) and, therefore, are equally far from us, yet often exhibiting a great difference in brightness. We know today that, of the three principal characteristics of a star — its mass, dimensions and luminosity — the last one exhibits by far the greatest dispersion. Yet this fact does not, by itself, invalidate Herschel's arguments on which his investigations of the galactic structure were based. For even if all stars are not of the same intrinsic brightness, the proposition that the fainter the star appears to be, the farther away it is, still remains statistically (even though not individually) true, though a proper account of the dispersion of the stellar luminosity function remained still a task for the future.

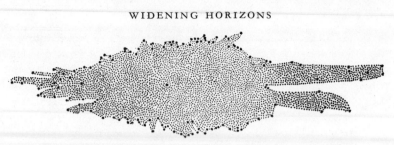

Fig. 17. The model of the Milky Way by William Herschel (1784).

In his studies of the galactic structure Herschel did not limit himself to mere counting of the stars of different apparent brightness, but in the course of his sweeps encountered many other objects which attracted his attention: namely, star clusters and nebulae. Again Herschel was not the first astronomer to notice them, for the nebulous object now known as the Great Nebula in Andromeda was detected by Simon Marius in 1612, and the well-known nebula in Orion was discovered by Cysat at Ingolstadt in 1619. Because those and others detected at an early date were often mistaken for comets, the well-known French comet hunter, Charles Messier (1730–1817), compiled in 1784 a list of 103 such objects to preclude their misidentification with comets.

Messier's catalogue soon reached Herschel (through the good offices of his Dr. Watson), and the objects listed in it became a favourite target for his telescopes. Already in 1784, he wrote to the German astronomer Bode in Berlin that his 20-foot telescope resolved almost all of Messier's 'nebulae' into clusters of stars; and no wonder that he thought eventually all to be so resolvable. In the course of his own sweeps of the sky, Herschel discovered altogether over 2500 clusters or nebular objects of this type, the positions of which he compiled in three separate catalogues published in 1786, 1795 and 1802.

In the early part of his career, inspired by his success in resolving most objects of Messier's catalogue, Herschel believed that there were only stars in the sky, organised in different types of stellar systems. One of these, our own Milky Way, contained our Sun with its family of planets. Other island-universes at moderate distance appear to us as star clusters; while the more distant ones we see as nebular clouds.

By 1791, Herschel's views on the nature of the nebulae had,

however, undergone a gradual change. He still regarded many of them as unresolved systems of stars, and among these, with a wonderful prescience, he placed the Andromeda nebula. But others, such as the one below Orion's belt, he now regarded as shining cloud of tenuous gas, forming a substrate from which stars are eventually formed. These conclusions were drawn from mere observations of telescopic appearances many decades before William Huggins found in 1864 that Herschel's two classes of nebulae exhibit also distinct types of spectra gaseous nebulae being characterized by spectra consisting of a limited number of bright emission lines, while the spectra of unresolved clusters of stars are mainly continuous.

On calculating how far off such clusters must be to escape resolution by his telescopes, Herschel concluded that they must lie far beyond the boundaries of our Milky Way as determined by his star gauges. And this led him to propose his celebrated theory of 'island-universes'—i.e., universes filled in with detached systems of stars, of which our own galactic system was but one. This was, perhaps, the highest point to which human cosmological thought had risen up to the commencement of the 19th century of our era, and also one whose follow-on was still almost a hundred years in the future.

That Herschel was fully aware of the vast expanse of the horizons which his life's work had opened up for human science is reflected in the remarks which the 75-year old astronomer made to the British poet, Thomas Campbell, who visited him in 1813: 'I have *looked further into space than ever human being did before me*. I have observed stars of which the light . . . must take two million years to reach the Earth. Nay more, if those distant bodies had ceased to exist millions of years ago, we should still see them, as the light did travel after their source was gone.'

Not all of Herschel's work attained the same heights of intellectual prowess or was guided by the same level of inspiration, and his views on the inhabitability of the Moon or even of the Sun are apt today to produce only a smile. Short of superhuman miracles, this could hardly have been otherwise. Like Johannes Kepler two centuries earlier, William Herschel was a seer—sleepwalker, if you wish—in certain areas of little-understood knowledge, but hopelessly lost in others. Like Kepler, Herschel too was given to the habit of jumping to conclusions in a way which, when it comes off, we describe as superior insight, and when it does not, we call wild-cat speculation. In this he was a contrast to the other great British astronomer of the half-century preceding Herschel's, James Bradley, who, when he discovered the nutation of the Earth's axis of rotation caused by lunar attraction, watched it for 18 years of its complete period before announcing its discovery. But astronomy needs at times an injection of an imagination such as Kepler's, or Herschel's, to lift it from a rut; and just as Kepler's new picture of the solar system rejuvenated celestial mechanics, Herschel's mind leaping ahead in cosmological speculation gave purpose to the observational campaign which his improvement of the telescope had made possible.

Herschel's glory and principal title to fame rests, however, on his accomplishments as an observer, and in looking over the enormous range of his observational exploits we can never cease to ask ourselves: how did Herschel succeed in accomplishing so much in the course of a career which did not commence until our astronomer was already middle-aged? The optical excellence of his instruments, far surpassing anything known up to that time, furnishes a part of the answer, but the personality of the observer must have been of equal importance.

In order to prove this, it is sufficient to ask what has been done with the other telescopes which Herschel made, with equal care, for others. About seventy of them are on record, but (with perhaps one exception) nothing astronomical seems to have been accomplished with them—a tribute to Herschel's genius as an observer rather than an aspersion on his ability as a telescope maker. The list of his customers (still preserved) partly explains this. It would obviously have been too much for any discoveries to be made with a 25-foot telescope furnished to the King of Spain, or by many other instruments ordered by such august customers as the Empress of Russia or the Emperor of Austria (orders undoubtedly stimulated by the patronage of George III; for it was evidently the fashion among royalty and nobility of that day to possess a Herschel telescope—as it later became to drive around in a Rolls Royce). But what was accomplished with two costly mirrors supplied by Herschel to the Greenwich Observatory, or with the one which went to Oxford? Nothing whatever commensurate with Herschel's discoveries.

Fig. 18.　　　　**WILLIAM HERSCHEL**
(1738–1822)

"Coelorum perrupit Claustra"

(A portrait by Artaud, of the astronomer at 81 years of age, reproduced by courtesy of the Royal Astronomical Society and of the Ronan Picture Library.)

For who else but Herschel among his contemporaries possesed the requisite skill and almost superhuman patience to use to full effect optically good but crudely mounted telescopes, and without any automatic drive to maintain an object in the field of view of an eyepiece magnifying more than a thousand times? In response to queries by one of his incredulous fellow-astronomers, Alexander Aubert, Herschel wrote playfully (on 9 January 1782) that ... 'these instruments have played me so many tricks that I have at last found them out in many of their humours, and have made them confess to me what they would have concealed if I had not with such per-severance and patience countered them. I have tortured them with powers, flattered them with attendance to find out the critical moments when they would act, tried them with specula of a short and of a long focus, a large aperture and a narrow one; it would be hard if they had not been kind to me at last'.

And, last but not least, let us remember that Herschel's entire observational work had to be accomplished under the open skies of southern England—without the benefit of any dome—at a time when the weather was certainly no different from what it is today, and clouds no less ubiquitous. This means that most of Herschel's work had to be made virtually through holes in the clouds, or during brief spells when the sky cleared up for an hour or so. The endless patient waiting for such breaks before the days of weather forecasts must have imposed an additional strain on the observer. Caroline Herschel, William's sister and indefatigable observing assistant for almost fifty years, related for us how her brother used to run out from the concert hall to his telescope during the inter-missions of concerts which he was conducting at Bath; and how years later when they moved to Datchet and ultimately to Slough, the ageing astronomer, with his eye hardly ever off the telescope, used to dictate to her what he saw while the ink was freezing in her inkstand. And no night was to be wasted under any circumstances! When they were moving from Clay Hall to Slough, Caroline related in a family letter '. . . the last night we spent under the open sky till dawn, occupied with comet seeking; and yet in the evening our instruments had to be ready for next night's work in the garden of our new house at Slough.' The name of this little village, until then known only to its neighbours, soon became the centre of astrono-mical world attention, like Palomar mountain was to become a century and a half later. In the words of François Arago, soon to become director of the Paris Observatory, 'in no other place in the world were so many discoveries made in so short a time as in that little house in Slough.'

This was, indeed, the heroic period of our science, the time of wooden telescopes used by men who had to have what it took to be an observer, a time gone by as gradual advances of engineering caught up with astronomical requirements. Perhaps as a reward for their exertions, observing astronomers of those days were often vouchsafed the gift of an unusually long life span. For William Herschel was almost 84 years of age when, after a brief illness, he was laid to his final rest, on 28 August 1822, in the country church in Upton by Windsor, under a tombstone reminding posterity that it was he who 'coelorum perrupit claustra'; having survived his royal patron, the erratic but benevolent King George III, by nearly two years. Moreover, his sister Caroline survived William by a full 26 years, and did not pass away until 9 January 1848 in Hanover (where she returned from England after William's death), two years after the discovery in Germany of another planet, Neptune, the existence of which was predicted by Adams in England and Leverrier in France from the gravitational perturbations of Uranus discovered by William Herschel 65 years earlier, on 13 March 1781, while the ever faithful Caroline, then in the full bloom of her youth, was at his side.

6 The Depths of the Universe

With the passing, in 1822, of William Herschel, an epoch came to a close, and its sequel was slow to unroll for several reasons. First, during his lifetime Herschel as an observer outdistanced his contemporaries so far that decades had to come and go before the main front of astronomical advance caught up with his earlier discoveries, and, it may be added, none of them were found to be incorrect in any essential respect*. His pioneer work in statistical astronomy set the course for his successors to follow throughout the entire 19th century, and the two problems raised, galactic star counts and determination of the solar motion through space, remained practically the sole occupations of stellar statisticians until Kapteyn's discovery of two star-streams in 1904.

And not only did the range of problems opened up by Herschel's work at the beginning of the 19th century not blossom out as widely as one could expect, but also his instrumental accomplishments failed to be followed up for a long time. In contrast with the period dominated by Herschel, astronomy of the 19th century could be characterized as one of precision and refined practice rather than of any spectacular advances which characterized the last decade of the 18th century. Theoretical astronomy in the 19th century became more than ever virtually identified with celestial mechanics, and the period extending from P. S. Laplace (1749–1827) to Henri Poincaré (1854–1912) saw some of its finest flowers blossom out in their autumnal beauty. On the instrumental side, the first great era of astronomical reflectors, which owed so much

---

* This was true even of Herschel's early estimates (in 1782) of the apparent angular diameters of the stars. These proved to correspond to the dimensions of the diffraction pattern of the apertures used by him, though their theory was still unknown in his time.

to the genius of William Herschel, spent also much of its momentum
—with the decline of the ageing astronomer—in the face of technical difficulties which were insuperable at that time. It is true that
isolated achievements of his successors in England, such as William
Lassell of Liverpool (1799–1880), who in 1852 erected and used a
50-inch reflector; or of Lord Rosse (1800–1867), whose Leviathan
reflector of 72-inches of free aperture completed in 1845 at Birr
Castle in Ireland revealed the spiral nature of the Andromeda nebula
to visual observation, command still today our attention and
respect. But these were not the types of instruments which impressed their particular mark on the astronomy of the 19th century.
Instead, the pendulum began to swing back from reflectors to
refractors, for reasons which deserve to be detailed in a few
words.

The underlying causes of this change of scenery were, as usual,
connected with contemporary developments in technology.
Thus by the beginning of the 19th century, Guinand in Switzer-
land, Feil, and others had at last mastered the art of producing
blocks of flint glass of necessary optical quality for the production
of achromatic objectives of increasing size, and these, at the hands
of Fraunhofer and of his successors, had rapidly secured ascendancy
to the refracting telescope as the primary tool of astronomical
research; and this ascendancy was to last for the rest of the
century.

The prototype of this type of instrument which rapidly pop-
ulated most observatories of the world was the $9\frac{1}{2}$-inch refractor
of 4 m focal length which Josef Fraunhofer (1787–1826) of
Munich, Germany, delivered in 1824 for the Dorpat Observatory
in Russia, and which, in the hands of F. G. W. Struve yielded the
determination of one of the first parallaxes of fixed stars (see p. 104).
The dimensions of this instrument were modest in comparison
with the reflectors of the Herschelian era, but their equatorial
mounting and, above all, mechanical driving clock offsetting the
effects of the diurnal rotation of the Earth, proved an inestimable
advantage. Yet even this new kind of telescope took a long time to
reach maturity; for even as late as 1865 the largest refractors
then in existence, at Pulkovo Observatory in Russia, and the
Harvard College Observatory in Cambridge, Mass., U.S.A.,
possessed objectives no larger than 15-inches in aperture. How-

ever, soon thereafter, refractors of ever-increasing size began to come out from the hands of Alvan Clark and his successors in Cambridge, Mass., culminating in the 40-inch refractor of the Yerkes Observatory near Chicago, U.S.A., completed in 1897. Today, seventy years later, this refractor still remains the largest of its kind, as a mute witness to the fact that once more the evolution of its line bogged down under its own weight—not because larger glass discs of requisite optical quality could not be made (they actually were) but rather because the absorption of light in glass of increasing thickness threatened to defeat their light-gathering power.

Astronomical refractors of the type just described, together with their smaller and more sedate brother called the 'meridian circle', dominated our observatories throughout the most part of the 19th century; and no shrine of Urania built in those days would have been complete without them. What did they contribute to our science? It we attempt to measure these contributions by the standards of novelty or originality to which we are now accustomed, the accomplishments of our 19th century grandfathers would, perhaps, appear on the surface to have been none too spectacular. Yet they were necessary at that time to pave the way for the future. Our astronomical grandfathers whose full beards flourished in the second half of the 19th century had, perhaps, a few if any intellectual giants among them; but they worked indefatigably laying fown the foundations for a more exciting future. It is to these Victorian grandfathers—ranging from the times of F. W. A. Argelander (1799–1875) to Arthur G. F. Auwers (1838–1915), Karl Friedrich Küstner (1856–1936) or Frank Schlesinger (1871–1943), arch-priests of exact astrometry—that we owe the principal catalogues of the positions of stars over the entire sky, the determination of several thousand stellar proper motions, and almost a hundred trigonometric parallaxes that were established by 1900, which provided the backbone for all subsequent penetrations into much greater depths of the Universe.

Photography and photometry made their debut on the astronomical scene likewise in the latter part of the 19th century, and spectroscopy appeared towards its end. But most astronomers of the 19th century were preoccupied with measurements of the positions of celestial bodies and their interpretation. Their principal ingenuity—as exemplified in the professional career of Friedrich Wilhelm Bessel (1784–1846), the greatest astronomer of the age immediately following Herschel's—was directed towards refinements of observational practice, and the endless struggle towards the improvements of the last decimals of the result. To give an example recapturing this attitude: Edward Charles Pickering (1846–1919), as a young director of Harvard Observatory, was roundly criticized by his senior Harvard colleague Benjamin O. Peirce (of *Short Table of Integrals* fame) for wasting the time of his staff on large-scale measurements of the brightness of the stars, a quantity measureable within errors of a few parts in a hundred, when he could be measuring stellar positions within errors of a few parts in a million! The nineteenth century produced in Carl Friedrich Gauss (1777–1855) a mathematician of the calibre of Archimedes or Newton, but, in astronomy, alas, Johannes Kepler or William Herschel would have found no compeer.

As a result, when the 19th century was drawing to a close, our knowledge of the structure of the Universe had not seemingly progressed very far beyond the stage at which William Herschel left it. In 1902 Simon Newcomb (1835–1909), a leading American astronomer of his day, put on record what he described as 'the wonderful advances of our generation in the knowledge of the fixed stars'. His book, *The Stars: A Study of the Universe*, depicted the material universe as a conglomeration of some hundreds of millions of stars rather strongly flattened in the galactic plane, with the clusters of the Milky Way forming a boundary girdle. As regards the size of 'that collection of stars which we call the Universe' Newcomb was rather noncommittal, but seemed to have had in mind a disc of some 10 000 light years in diameter. He realized that these dimensions would appear unduly grandiose to many astronomers, and was chiefly concerned to defend them against smaller estimates.

And ten years later? Listen to this: 'Direct evidence on whether the spiral nebulae are within or without our stellar system is completely lacking. The mere fact that the spiral nebulae shun the galaxy may indicate that they are influenced by it'. And this: 'If spiral nebulae are within the stellar system, we have no notion of what their structure may be . . . If, however, they are external to the stellar system we have at least a hypothesis that can be followed up

. . . If each spiral nebula is a stellar system, it follows that our own system is a spiral nebula.'

No, that was not written by William Herschel or his son John a century or more before. These were quotations from a book entitled *Stellar Movements and the Structure of the Universe* (1914) with which Arthur Stanley Eddington (1882–1944) commenced a career that led him to the front rank among astronomers in the first half of the 20th century. And here is another excerpt from the same book: 'The distance of the Lesser Magellanic Cloud is found to be 10 000 parsecs (30 000 light years)—the greatest distance that we have yet had occasion to mention.' Or 'The whole number of nebulae bright enough to be photographed has been estimated . . . at 160 000.' This was the picture which the explorers of the Universe had before them but little more than fifty years ago!

The change—explosive change, the greatest yet in the age-long history of our subject—in this time-honoured picture of the Universe around us has taken place since that time, and we still find ourselves spell-bound right in the midst of it. The reason why this veritable explosion of our knowledge was so sudden is no new or more profound theoretical insight born in the brain of a philosopher. It was the dramatically new observational evidence, furnished by current advances of human technology, which confronted us forcibly with new horizons of incredible vastness. The greatest expansion of our cosmic horizons which our thought is still trying to comprehend with difficulty occurred indeed within our lifetime, and in what follows we shall endeavour to trace its principal outlines.

The beginning of the course leading us straight into the present rapids can be traced with relative precision, and is largely symbolized in the person of George Ellery Hale (1868–1936) who more than any single individual stands at its source. The story of the way in which this outstanding young scientist, embodying the best of the Yankee enterprising spirit of his time, left in 1904 the newly founded Yerkes Observatory (for which Hale secured the 40-inch refractor) to turn with a small band of dedicated followers to the lofty heights of Mount Wilson in southern California in quest of better skies—an exodus which was to open veritably a new chapter in the history of astronomy—has its rightful place side by side with the romance of William Herschel. Largely as a result of this move, after the opening years of this century the pendulum of progress began to swing once more from refractors to reflectors, for the twilight of refracting telescopes went hand in hand with a new triumph for astronomical reflectors which continue to reign supreme in our observatories today—from the 60-inch reflector erected at Mt. Wilson in 1908, to the 200-inch glass giant of Palomar Mountain dedicated in 1948—and the Goliath of them all, the new Russian 236-inch reflector now being erected in the mountains of the Caucasus.* In particular, in the past 25 years reflectors with apertures in excess of 60 inches have begun to multiply in many parts of the world, that scarcely a year elapses now before there are new additions to their list.

The relative ease with which optics for these large reflectors can now be produced, mounted and controlled, has led to an unparalleled increase in celestial light-gathering power within our lifetime. Whereas by 1900 the total light-gathering area of the objectives of all refractors used for scientific work did not exceed some 14 000 square inches, by 1960 this has increased to 247 000 sq. inches—an almost eighteenfold increase in 60 years—though still only equivalent to that of a single telescope of 560-inch free aperture. This increase in celestial light-gathering power is one of the principal reasons why we have been able to learn more about astronomy in the past sixty years than all our ancestors found out in as many preceding centuries!

The mere gathering of light of the celestial bodies is, to be sure, only the first step of astronomical research; for all depends on what we do with it once we have captured it in the focal planes of our telescopes. In point of fact, whenever we wish to study the properties of any celestial body inaccessible to direct approach, all the information we can hope to obtain must reach us across the intervening gap of space through two different channels: namely, the gravitational attraction, and the radiation (electromagnetic or corpuscular). And, we may add, the messages reaching us from a distance through these channels are, in these days of increasing

---

* The reader may be interested to learn that this latest Leviathan among astronomical telescopes, which may well remain the largest ever to be erected and operated on the surface of the Earth (as its successors are likely to be launched into orbit), has been provided with the azimuthal rather than parallactic mounting—i.e., in much the same way as William Herschel's 40-foot telescope of 1789, only in a mechanically much more satisfactory manner.

specialization, analysed and interpreted by astronomers of very different interests and training. Gravitational attraction controls the motion of the celestial bodies, manifesting itself in the continuous changes of their positions with time. Both position and time can be measured by modern techniques to a very high accuracy and, moreover, the laws of nature relating the position with time are well known and understood. As a result, the scholars concerned with them are inclined to be of the austere type, who always know what they are doing, and their professional efforts are, in general, bent on improving the last decimals of their results.

Astronomers concerned with the study of light are, on the whole, a very different lot. Their measurements can seldom as yet be made more accurate than to about one part in a thousand and, to make matters worse, the laws of light emission (or its interaction with matter) are much more complicated. As a result, in order to squeeze information from light, astrophysicists can no longer just look at it, as in the days of Galileo Galilei or of William Herschel, and merely describe what they see; for hard experience taught them that the human eye itself is a notoriously unreliable tool and that its sensitivity is rather seriously limited. Instead, in order to extract the desired information, they have to treat light captured by their telescopes in a way reminiscent of the medieval torture chambers. The captive waves of light—those nimble-footed messengers reaching us from distant worlds across the intervening gaps of space—are made to pass through prisms, or to bounce off gratings, to be decomposed into a spectrum. Or they must reduce silver grains of photographic emulsions; to heat the joints of thermocouples or, worse still, by the intermediary of a photosensitive surface they are converted into an electric current and sent down the wire to operate the pen of automatic recording instruments. This is what the astrophysicist must needs do in order to extract from the light of distant cosmic bodies all information he desires to know about them; and will not be satisfied until he has converted all of it into clusters of silver grains on photographic plates, or to various curves recorded by a pen driven by photocurrents. And of these, determinations of the brightness of distant celestial light sources, and of their spectra, proved to be of greatest importance for further penetration into really deep space, by methods which we shall now proceed to outline.

Up to the end of the 19th century our knowledge of the distances of the Universe around us still hinged on trigonometric determination of stellar parallaxes discussed already in Chapter IV, and by 1900 such parallaxes had been determined by absolute measurements for approximately 100 stars, mostly within 10 parsecs away from us. An introduction of photographic methods for determination of relative parallaxes (i.e., of the measurement of parallactic shifts of nearby stars relative to the neighbouring fainter, and therefore, presumably more distant, objects) after 1900 by Schlesinger and others led eventually to a penetration into space down to distances of the order of 100 parsecs. But beyond there any further progress was inseparably connected with the development of other—photometric—methods for the determination of cosmic distances. Such methods, which have been our principal tool for the exploration of the Universe in the past fifty years, are no longer based on direct regular measures of any parallactic displacements (though their calibration still depends indirectly upon them) just as our penetration into the realm of nearby stars by measurements of trigonometric parallaxes depended on the previous mensuration of the size of our terrestrial orbit around the Sun.

In the first decade of the 20th century we began systematically to learn more about the stars than the distance of some, or of the apparent brightness of a great many more; for advancing techniques enabled us to measure also their colour, or to develop their light into spectra. A combination of such data not only confirmed the fact, known already to William Herschel, that the stars differ greatly among themselves in their intrinsic (absolute) brightness or luminosity, but disclosed an even more interesting fact: namely, that the absolute luminosity of at least some types of stars is significantly correlated with their colour or spectral characteristics. This discovery, first made by the great Danish astronomer Einar Hertzsprung (1873–1967) in 1905, became the cornerstone for the determinations of so-called 'spectroscopic parallaxes', which were based on estimates of the absolute luminosity of the stars from the characteristics of their spectra, and subsequent computation of the distances at which such stars must be in order to appear to us as faint as they do. This method of 'spectroscopic parallaxes' enabled us to push the limits of the fathomable Universe from a few dozen parsecs attainable trigonometrically to a few thousand parsecs, and up to the present time, distances of some 6000 individual stars have been estimated in this manner.

But it was not stars shining with constant light that proved to be our best tools for deeper penetration into space. Much more powerful tools to this end have been provided by certain types of 'variable stars'. That not all stars in the sky shine with constant light has been known to astronomers for a long time. Their first representative, the well-known Mira Ceti in the constellation of the Whale, was discovered by Fabricius in 1596, still in the days of pre-telescopic astronomy; and the variability of Algol in the Head of Medusa (held by Perseus), noticed by Montanari in 1670, led to the discovery of a prototype of what we call now 'eclipsing binaries'. But it was not till the discovery of the variability of the star δ Cephei by Goodricke in 1784 that a prototype was discovered of the class of variables which were to play such an important role in our far-flung exploits of deep space from the beginning of the 20th century.

Unlike Mira-like objects, variable stars akin to δ Cephei ('cepheids' as we are accustomed to call them) vary but moderately in light (seldom by more than $1\frac{1}{2}$ magnitudes between maximum and minimum). But they do so in a characteristic manner which makes them easy to distinguish, and with clock-like regularity in periods which range from several hours to several days. By 1900 several dozens of these had been discovered in various parts of the sky; but this was nothing in comparison with what was to follow later.

By 1912, Miss Henrietta Swan Leavitt (1868–1921), working at Harvard Observatory on photographic plates of Magellanic clouds (nebular objects discovered near the celestial southern pole by early circumnavigators, which were later resolved into stars by powerful telescopes), identified in their stellar population a large number of stars varying in light in a manner similar to δ Cephei, and noted also one interesting fact: namely, that the brightness of each such object appeared to be the greater, the longer the period of its light variations. By their conspicuous concentration in the Magellanic cloud, these variables were obviously a part of it; but as the dimensions of this cloud constitute but a very small fraction of its distance from us, the apparent magnitudes of all stars imbedded in it could differ only by a constant from their absolute magnitudes measuring intrinsic brightness.

Therefore, what Miss Leavitt actually discovered was the fact that a cepheid whose light varies in a given period—and this period can be ascertained from observations with relative ease—possesses a certain definite absolute brightness; and if the latter could be established, a difference between the absolute and apparent brightness could be used as an indication of the distance of the respective star. In other words, if we could calibrate the relation found by Miss Leavitt to exist between the period and apparent brightness of cepheids in the Magellanic clouds by establishing the absolute brightness of a cepheid in our proximity of any period, a powerful tool would be obtained for calculating distances of all systems containing cepheids from the measured apparent brightness of such variables of a given period.

Unfortunately, all cepheid variables in our own galactic system are beyond the reach of a direct triangulation of their annual parallaxes. However, many of those of short period were found to exhibit measurable proper motions, and from a discussion of their 'parallactic' components (see p. 118) Hertzsprung deduced in 1913 the absolute magnitude of short-period cepheids (i.e., with periods less than a day) to be close to $0^{m}.0$ on the international scale—a result which withstood several re-examinations until 1952, when Baade found that for 'classical' cepheids, the zero-point was actually brighter by 1.5 magnitudes. It was, however, Hertzsprung's zero-point which led to Eddington's estimate of the distance of the Magellanic cloud we quoted on p. 132.

This new method of the determination of 'photometric parallaxes' is made even more effective by the fact that cepheid variables of long period belong among absolutely very bright stars—i.e., constitute 'standard candles' or, rather, powerful cosmic beacons distinguishable across vast expanses of space. With normal stars, this is much less certain. If we look at the sky at night with the naked eye or through a telescope, it is as difficult to estimate the distance from their brightness as to guess the distance of shore lights from a ship. During the night the lights visible at sea are many, but our estimate of their distance may be off by many orders of magnitude if we take for a ship the light of a setting planet or a star. But maybe we can see on the horizon a light which flashes and disappears at regular time intervals. This sequence of luminous dots and dashes will tell us that we are watching a light-house, and we can estimate its distance quite well if we know the candle-power of its lights— provided, of course, that there is no fog! And what is true at sea, is true in the sky. The stars we see there may appear to be of different brightness because some are nearer to us than others, or because of differences in their intrinsic luminosity. But if we spot a star which changes light, like δ Cephei, in a period of $5\frac{1}{2}$ days, we know that this particular star must be 2800 times intrinsically brighter than our Sun; and similarly for cepheids with other periods of their light changes.

This 'period-luminosity relation' of cepheid variables soon became a tool of fundamental importance for the exploration of more remote parts of the Universe, and the first major advance scored with its aid was made in the field of galactic structure. Up to 1915, the system of our own Milky Way was still regarded to conform to the 'Herschel-Kapteyn' model of a flattened system of stars, some 12 000 light years across and 3000 light years thickness, with stars concentrated towards the plane of the Galaxy and towards its centre. The Sun with its system of planets was supposed to be located in the central parts of this system, thus occupying (for the last time in the history of astronomy) some kind of special position.

However, it has been known for a long time that the belt of the Milky Way in the sky is accompanied by a little more than one hundred dense compact groups of stars, well described by the term 'globular clusters'. A good many of these were known already to Messier in the 18th century, and resolved into stars by the powerful telescopes of William Herschel. A search for variable stars in globular clusters in the last part of the 19th century led to the discovery, in most of them, of short-period cepheids in numbers so large (the cluster ω Centauri is known to contain over 200 of them) as to have earned them the epithet of 'cluster-type variables'. Since 1913 these variables became the principal tools for determination of the distances of clusters in which they are imbedded.

This work was systematically undertaken between 1915–1918 at Mt. Wilson Observatory by Harlow Shapley (1885–   ) with truly remarkable results. It was known even before this time that the distribution of globular clusters along the belt of the Milky Way was highly asymmetric—in point of fact, all of them are situ-

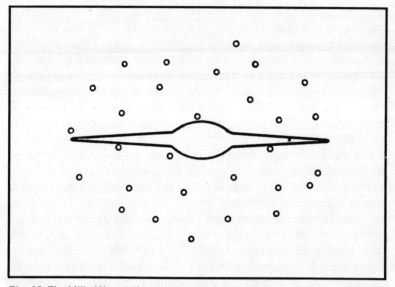

Fig. 19. The Milky Way and its associated system of Globular Clusters (schematic).

ated on one hemisphere of the sky, centered on the Milky Way clouds in the southern constellation of Sagittarius—but their distances from us as determined from the apparent brightness of their cluster-type variables turned out to be of the order of tens of thousands of light years. Moreover, when Shapley constructed the spatial model of the system of globular clusters, he found it to lie in the constellation of Sagittarius (at a galactic longitude of $l = 325°$)some 50 000 light years from the Sun. This point Shapley boldly identified with the centre of the entire Milky Way system, consisting of a flat disc of stars surrounded by a spherical agglomeration of globular clusters, and in this he was indeed right. As a result of Shapley's work, our Galaxy began to emerge to the astronomer's minds for what it actually is: a gigantic system of stars, some ten times larger than all its earlier estimates from Herschel to Kapteyn made it out to be, with our Sun located eccentrically some 15 000 parsecs from its centre. In one stroke did we thus lose by Shapley's work the last vestige of any claim to a privileged position in the Universe, and our Sun became only one of some 10^{12} other stars constituting our Galaxy.

The dimensions of our Galaxy as deduced by Shapley were, to

be sure, somewhat overestimated; for in 1918 Shapley knew nothing as yet of the role which a concentration of gas and dust close to the galactic plane exerts in dimming light of distant objects of low galactic latitude. The role of this 'interstellar fog' was not realized more fully till as a result of Trumpler's work on galactic clusters in 1930; and when due account was taken for interstellar absorption, Shapley's distance to the centre of the Galaxy diminished from 50 000 to 30 000 light years—in substantial agreement with all subsequent work.

For the dimensions of our Galaxy were soon to be determined by another method connected with its dynamical characteristics. That a Galaxy as our fathers saw it at the beginning of this century cannot represent a stationary system of stars moving at random, but that its flattened form must be due to axial rotation about its shorter axis, was already clear to Henri Poincaré in his *Leçons sur les Hypothèses Cosmogoniques* (1908), on general dynamical grounds. However, the way in which such a rotation would leave a specific imprint in the proper motions and radial velocities of the stars in our neighbourhood was not investigated until by Bertil Lindblad (1892–1965) in 1926, and by Jan H. Oort (1900–   ) a year later. The first indications of the rotation of the galactic wheel were pointed out by E. F. Freundlich and E. von den Pahlen already in 1922; but it was not until the work of Lindblad and Oort that differential motions of nearby stars were made to reveal their rotational motion around the centre of our Galaxy. This centre was located in almost the same position deduced by Shapley from his study of the globular star clusters ($l = 328°$), but at a distance of 8200 parsecs (27 000 light years). The Galaxy was, moreover, found to rotate not like a rigid wheel, but with an angular velocity increasing towards its centre. At the distance of the Sun, one revolution around the galactic centre (i.e., the so-called 'cosmic year') lasts about 200 million years of our terrestrial time. Therefore, when the Sun with its planetary system last occupied the same relative position with respect to the galactic centre as now, our Earth was in the Triassic period of the Mesozoic age—the age at which great reptiles were about to emerge from the swamps to take over solid land but recently liberated from the Permian ice-age. And in another cosmic year—who knows?

But before we strain our gaze too far into the future, let us look around our sky in quest of formations which may take us deeper in space today. We mentioned already in the preceding chapter that William Herschel, in his sweeps of the sky, noted the existence of a great many nebular patches which defied resolution into stars with telescopes, but which he nevertheless suspected to be distant 'island-universes'; and of these, the well-known nebula in Andromeda was a typical example. This suspicion was strengthened in the 19th century when such nebulae were found to exhibit spectra akin to those of the stars, in contrast to the bright-line spectra of other nebulae consisting of tenuous gas. Moreover, the largest telescopes of the 19th century—such as the 72-inch Leviathan of Lord Rosse—disclosed that 'nebulae' akin to the one in Andromeda exhibit indications of spiral structure. The advent of photographs confirmed this structure for many more objects of this class.

What was, however, the size of such objects and where were they located in space? Did they belong to our own galactic system, or were they extragalactic? For almost the entire first quarter of the 20th century the answer still hung in the balance, with seemingly valid reasons being advanced in favour of each one of the opposing views. The question was, in particular, debated in public between 1919–1921 by Heber D. Curtis (1872–1942) defending the extragalactic position of spiral nebulae, and Harlow Shapley opposing it on grounds which the historian of science will still find of interest today—as a reflection of the perplexities which beset our astronomical ancestors of that time.

As has happened only too often both before and since, the principal contributory factors which controlled contemporary views were the telescopes, rather than the astronomers at their ends. The year of 1917, while Europe was in the midst of the grim drama of the First World War, witnessed the inauguration, in California, of the 100-inch telescope at Mount Wilson—a bigger brother to the 60-inch of 1908, and the largest telescope created by human hand since the completion of Lord Rosse's 72-inch instrument more than seventy years before. The 100-inch Hooker telescope became the crowning optical achievement of George Willis Ritchey (1864–1946) and a monument truly "aere perennius"; for no other telescope has contributed more new knowledge to astronomy during the first half-century of its existence.

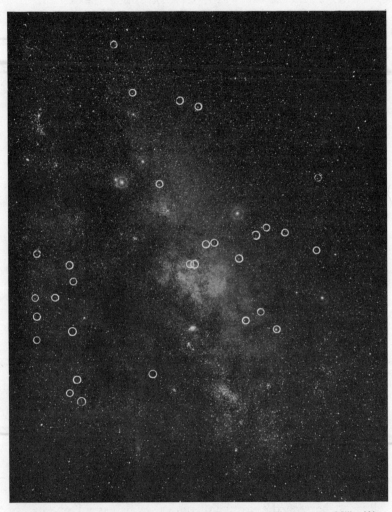

Fig. 20. A wide-angle photograph of the Sagittarius Clouds in the Milky Way, concealing the centre of our galactic system. The circles indicate the positions of the individual globular clusters surrounding the centre of the Galaxy.

Fig. 21. A typical globular star cluster ω Centauri (N.G.C. 5139) in the southern sky—rich in cluster-type variables—seen at a distance of some 7000 parsecs (22,000 light years), and photographed from the southern station of Harvard Observatory in Bloemfontein, South Africa.

Fig. 22. The Great Nebula in Andromeda (M31 NGC 224) with its companions—
one of the two neighbouring spiral galaxies at a distance of a little more than
two million light years—a close twin of our own galactic system, indicating
what we should look like to an observer in space (Lick Observatory photograph).

Fig. 23. Beyond the confines of the local group of galaxies—comprising the Andromeda or Triangulum nebulae as well as our own Milky Way system—at a distance of not less than six million light years hovers the spiral galaxy Messier 81 in the constellation of Ursa Maior. (Photograph was taken with the 100-inch reflector of the Mount Wilson Observatory in California, U.S.A.)

One of the first feats of this new giant eye with which astronomers began to watch the sky in 1917 was the resolution of the central parts of the nebulae in Andromeda (M31) and Triangulum (M33) into individual stars—a feat which had previously defied William Herschel as well as Lord Rosse. And more than that: for among the multitude of stars into which these nebulae began to be resolved, Curtis and Duncan discovered a number of so-called temporary stars or 'novae'—stars which, at a certain stage of their evolutionary course, undergo spasmodic outbursts of light, rendering them temporarily (for time intervals of days or weeks) as bright intrinsically as the brightest normal stars shining with constant light. Such 'new' stars have long been familiar to us from our own Galaxy, where they attain at maximum a known and fairly constant absolute magnitude. If, now, similar novae discovered by Curtis and Duncan in the Andromeda nebula attained the same absolute brightness, this nebula must be at a distance of not less than 270 000 parsecs (some 900 000 light years)—i.e., clearly extragalactic, and of a size comparable with our Milky Way system.

Such a view was, however, contested at that time by Harlow Shapley, who (like Eddington before) was impressed with the fact that spiral nebulae are found to occur preferentially in the regions of the sky near the galactic poles, and avoid completely the galactic belt. From this Shapley concluded that formations exhibiting such a distribution must somehow be associated with our Galaxy. Besides, even if the Andromeda nebula were at the distance assigned to it by Curtis, it would still appear to be much smaller than our Milky Way system, and thus scarcely a fitting counterpart of our Galaxy.

These arguments, in which plausible reasons were advanced by both sides, were resolved in 1924 when Edwin P. Hubble (1889–1953)—soon to become the leading investigator of distant galaxies—discovered long-period cepheid variables in the Andromeda nebula with the 100-inch telescope at Mount Wilson; and the measured apparent brightness of these celestial 'standard candles' soon settled conclusively that the 'nebulae' in which these cepheids are imbedded are indeed definitely extragalactic. Shapley's arguments to the contrary, reasonable as they appeared to be in 1920, failed for reasons which did not become clear until a later time. The real reason why the galactic belt constitutes a 'zone of avoid-

ance' for spiral nebulae is the heavy absorption of light by interstellar matter which is concentrated in the galactic plane*. We
know already (cf. p. 140) that the disregard of this absorption led
Shapley to overestimate the dimensions of our galactic system by
one-third. Moreover, when Walter Baade (1893–1960), a leading
student of the galaxies in the post-Hubble era in which the primary
instrument of exploration since 1948 became the 200-inch telescope
at Palomar Mountain, corrected the calibration of the period-
luminosity curve for cepheid variables in 1952, the actual distance
of the Andromeda nebula was increased to 725 000 parsecs
(2 360 000 light years), and, at this distance, this neighbouring
galaxy proved almost a twin in size to our own.

Although the controversy about the internal versus external
location of spiral nebulae was virtually settled by Hubble in 1924,
it took almost 30 years to explain satisfactorily all the remaining
aspects of the problem raised in the Curtis-Shapley debates. The
reader should take note of the fact that the extragalactic nature of
spiral nebulae, though suspected since the days of William
Herschel, was not actually proven until less than 50 years ago. So
close do we live to this particular milestone which opened up the
way to scientific exploration of extra-galactic space!

This exploration really commenced somewhat earlier than 1924,
and from an unexpected direction, with spectroscopic studies of
the motions of external galaxies in the line of sight. Low-dispersion
spectra of several spiral nebulae were taken by Huggins and others
already during the 19th century (the fact that the spectrum of the
Andromeda nebula is similar to that of our Sun was established by
Scheiner in 1899), and these helped to distinguish them from
clouds or streaks of luminescent gas within our own Galaxy. However, the first investigator who set out systematically to study the
radial velocities of spiral nebulae by measuring the Doppler shifts
of their spectral lines was Vesto M. Slipher (1875–   ) in 1912 at
the Lowell Observatory in Flagstaff, Arizona. Between 1912 and
1914 Slipher succeeded in measuring spectroscopically such radial
velocities of 13 external galaxies accessible to his 24-inch reflector.
He found, to his surprise, that not only were these velocities about
ten times as large as for most ordinary stars, but that, in the case of

---

* Though 'windows' through it have been discovered in several places.

every single object investigated by him, red-shifted spectral lines pointed to a systematic recession of these nebulae from us, with velocities of the order of 100 km/sec. Between 1916–1917, F. G. Pease (1881–1938) at Mount Wilson found much the same to be true for many other objects of this class.

No sooner than these facts became known, astronomers began to analyse them for the relative motion of our own Galaxy among the rest; and it was the German astronomer Carl Wirtz (1876–1939) who first pointed out in 1924 that if the red shifts measured in the spectra of extragalactic nebulae are Doppler shifts indicative of radial motions, these nebulae recede from us at a rate which increases with their distance. This bold suggestion was not readily accepted by all students of this subject—among contemporary astronomers, Lundmark and Strömberg were plainly noncommittal—and the matter hung in suspense for five years until Hubble confirmed in 1929 that Wirtz's suggestion was indeed well-founded.

By 1929 Hubble knew no more radial velocities of spiral nebulae than Wirtz did five years earlier. However, two new factors enabled Hubble to decide the question. The first was the discovery of the galactic rotation in 1926–27, which disclosed our Sun to revolve around the centre of our Galaxy in a mildly eccentric orbit with a velocity close to 250 km/sec (155 mls/sec). A knowledge of this velocity enabled Hubble to reduce the observed 'heliocentric' radial velocities of spiral nebulae into 'galactocentric' ones, in much the same way as radial velocities of the stars observed from the revolving terrestrial platform are reduced to their heliocentric values. Secondly, on the basis of his own photometric work with the 100-inch reflector, Hubble obtained much better estimates of the distances of the nebulae with known radial velocities; and when he plotted this velocity against distance, he obtained a straight line suggesting the red shift (i.e., velocity of recession) to be proportional to the cosmic distance of the source—a statement which has since been generally known under the name of Hubble's Law.

From 1929, measurements of the red shifts in the spectra of extragalactic nebulae of increasing distance was taken up at Mount Wilson by Milton L. Humason (1891–   ), who, since 1936, had been joined in this quest by Nicholas U. Mayall (1906–   ) at Lick

Observatory. In the meantime, Shapley at Harvard and Hubble at Mount Wilson continued with their photometric work; Shapley concentrating on the exploration of the 'inner metagalaxy'—a group of extragalactic systems, small and large, within approximately 10 million parsecs from us—while Hubble, using the most powerful telescope of his age, pressed his search relentlessly into greater depths of the Universe.

It had been known for a long time that the number of nebulae in the sky which appeared to be extra-galactic was very large. James E. Keeler estimated by 1900 that the number of those within photographic reach of the 36-inch Crossley reflector of Lick Observatory exceeded one hundred thousand. With the advent of the large reflectors of the 20th century this number began to grow almost beyond any limit. Moreover, it was soon realized that these nebulae are not uniformly distributed all over the sky (not only because of the galactic belt blotted out by interstellar absorption), but occur preferentially in clusters of a few dozen to several hundreds of galaxies—clusters which constitute local dynamical systems (akin to our own 'inner metagalaxy') separated by great abysses of void.

All extragalactic nebulae outside our own 'inner metagalaxy' are much too far to be resolved into stars with even the most powerful telescopes at our disposal. However, the individual brightness of the brightest members of each cluster of nebulae can still be measured; and if we assume that their intrinsic brightness is equal to that of our own Milky Way or of the Andromeda nebula, the distance of the entire cluster can be calculated (again on the assumption that light suffers no extinction on its way across the depths of space). In this way, Hubble and others identified clusters of galaxies (veritable 'island universes') in the constellation of Ursa Maior at a distance of some 180 million light years, in Corona Borealis, at 250 million light years, and one in Bootes at 460 million light years. By 1936, when Hubble summarized his life's work in his well-known book *The Realm of Nebulae*, he believed he penetrated with his investigators the Universe down to a distance from which light has to travel for 500 million years to reach us, and yet subsequent work by Baade in 1952 has shown that even these enormous distances should still be doubled!

Therefore, while by the year 1700 astronomers had only just

Fig. 24. *The Depths of the Universe.* A cluster of distant extragalactic nebulae in the constellation of Ursa Maior. An arrow points to an external galaxy N.G.C. 4884 at a distance of some 300 million light years, exhibiting a red shift of spectral lines indicative of a velocity of recession in excess of 11,000 km/sec (6832 mls/sec). (Photographed by Walter Baade with the 60-inch reflector at the Mount Wilson Observatory in California.)

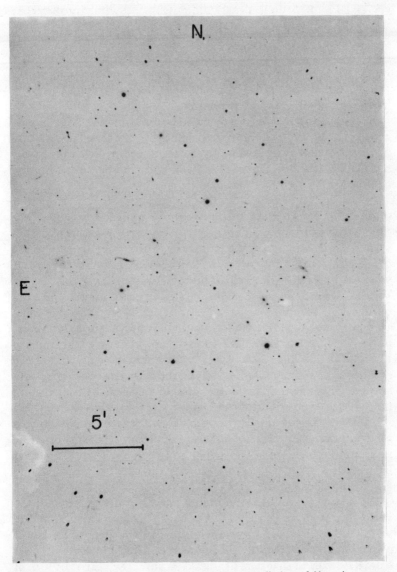

Fig. 25. A cluster of external galaxies in the constellation of Hercules—at an approximate distance of 300 million light years. (Photographed by F. Zwicky with the 200-inch telescope of Mt. Palomar Observatory in California.)

learned the distance separating us from the Sun (and equal to one traversed by light in less than 8 minutes), and while by 1800 they were still unable actually to measure the distance of one light year, by 1900 the dimensions of the Universe as known at that time increased to about 10 000 light years, and to 1 000 000 000 light years by the mid-twentieth century! These values would have mortified Pascal; but contemporary astronomers are accustomed to view them with much greater equanimity.

Even these figures did not prove to be the last word. Now, barely 20 years later, we have reason to believe that our actual penetration of the Universe may be almost ten times greater—thanks to the recent discovery of a new class of enigmatic objects in the sky, commonly referred to as *quasars*.

In order to give a brief account of this exciting story in the history of our subject, we must return twenty or more years back to the time when astronomers began to survey the sky with radio-telescopes capable of recording radiation in the microwave domain of the electromagnetic spectrum. This became possible after 1945, with the expertise gathered from radar work during the Second World War and put subsequently to a more peaceful use. When the outlines of the radio maps of the sky began dimly to emerge from accumulating records, they seemingly bore at first little or no relation to the heavens as we have known them from time immemorial. Like the sky visible to our eyes, in the microwave domain of the spectrum the sky disclosed, however, the existence of an increasing number of discrete radio sources standing out of the background noise. But the positions of these radio 'stars' failed to show at first any trace of a correlation with any visible objects, as though the two kinds of skies had virtually nothing in common. In fact, very few radio sources seem to be stellar at all, as interferometric techniques have shown them to possess angular dimensions incomparably larger than those of the stars.

Gradually, however, a continuing quest for identification of the radio sources with optical objects began to bear fruit. Thus the so-called Cassiopeia A—the strongest radio source of the sky—proved to be identical with the remnant of a supernova which must have flared up in that part of the sky around the year 1700 A.D. at a distance of some 10 000 light years, in so heavily an obscured region of the Milky Way (absorbing light, but not radio waves) that it completely escaped detection by astronomers at that time. Only faint nebular wisps, expanding with a velocity of some 7400 km/sec (4600 mls/sec), now mark the place of this catastrophe. Other known historical supernovae, such as the Chinese super-nova of 1054 A.D. (the remnants of which are now seen as the Crab Nebula) or Tycho's star of the year 1572, were also all found to be associated with known discrete radio sources. On the other hand, Cygnus A, the second strongest known radio source in the con-stellation of the Swan, was identified with a pair of colliding extra-galactic spiral nebulae, situated at a stupendous distance of 500 million light years.

By 1960, the prolonged patient efforts of the radio-astronomers working in conjunction with the optical astronomers—among whom Rudolf Minkowski (1895–   ), Alan Sandage (1926–   ) and Maarten Schmidt (1929–   ) of Mount Wilson and Palomar Observatories came to occupy an especially prominent place—led to the identification of about 300 discrete radio sources with specific optical objects. Of these, about half were found to be radio galaxies (similar to Cygnus A), and an appreciable fraction of the rest were objects described as 'quasistellar'. One of them, in particular, was destined to make history: namely, No. 273 of the *Third Catalogue of Radio Sources,* prepared in 1955 by Martin Ryle (1918–   ) and his colleagues at Cambridge. The position of this particular object in the sky could be determined with great precision on account of the fortunate fact that, very occasionally, this source undergoes occultation by the Moon. This happened in 1962, and a determina-tion of its disappearance and reappearance enabled Hazard, Mackay and Shimmins in Australia to fix its position even better than by use of any radio interferometer. And when Minkowski turned the 200-inch telescope to this part of the sky, he found in the place indicated by the radio-observers a faint bluish star-like object of 12.8th apparent magnitude—the brightest of all known 'quasars' (an acronym for quasi-stellar discrete radio sources).

At first no one had any idea of the distance of this enigmatic object—whether it was inside the galaxy, or extragalactic. Then in 1963 Maarten Schmidt obtained the spectrum of this 'quasar', and found its lines to be shifted to the red to such an extent that, if Hubble's linear relation between red shift and distance remains applicable, the observed red shift of 3C 273 would correspond to a distance of $1\frac{1}{2}$ milliard light years, rendering this quasar the most distant cosmic object in the Universe known up to that time!

Since 1963, red shifts have been measured for about 30 additional quasars, and 3C 273 would still seem to be one of the nearest. The greatest red shifts were observed so far for 3C 9, or for No. 1116, +12 of the *Australian Catalogue*, which a linear extrapolation of Hubble's Law would place to incomprehensible distances of more than 8 milliard light years! Moreover, if the observed red shifts of these objects were due to the Doppler effect, their magnitude would signify that these quasars are receding from us at a velocity equal to 80-81 per cent of that of light, and that their radiation reaching us now must have been almost half way en route by the time when our Earth was formed.

Furthermore, if all distant galaxies receding from us at such frantic speeds were formed at approximately the same time as our own system of the Milky Way, we should see them as they were when their light arriving now left them hundreds, or even thousands, of millions of years ago. In other words, the deeper we look into the Universe, the deeper we should penetrate into its distant past, and our giant telescopic eyes peering into these depths may provide us with an image of what our own Galaxy (and its neighbours) once looked like in the very distant past. This is due to the fact that communications in the Universe are not instantaneous, and that the waves of light—those nimble-footed messengers which alone offer communication service across vast gaps of space —travel at a finite speed.

But when they finally arrive at the Earth after free flights of millions, or hundreds of millions, of years and are intercepted by our observing instruments, are they still in their pristine state (so that the observer in the system they have left behind would still see them as light of the same colour) or did they get tired on the way and lose, perchance, a part of their energy in flight? In other words, are the stupendous red shifts of spectral lines in the light of cosmic objects at increasing distance really due to the Doppler effect caused by their recession, or to some other cause as yet unknown?

At present there appears to be no obvious reason to doubt the Doppler nature of the red shifts, or the validity of Hubble's law as an indicator of distance. However, it is also true that this constitutes so far only the simplest assumption, which lacks any independent confirmation. Within the solar system, in our Galaxy, the Doppler nature of spectral shifts is amply attested by independent evidence; but at cosmic distances amounting to hundreds of millions of years, who knows? It is true that theoretical physics offers so far no support for an alternative view that the energy of photons travelling freely through space may decay slowly over long intervals of time, and thus produce, perhaps, 'cosmological red shifts' of a different kind, which may superpose upon pure Doppler shifts due to recession.

The absence of theoretical guidance at this stage need not, however, mean too much, for like astronomy, physics too is in a constant state of flux and its history should teach us to keep an open mind. How often in the past did our scientific ancestors jump to conclusions to solve the riddle of the Sphinx, only to be shown to have misconceived the meaning of her smile at the next turn of the flow of our river of knowledge? No investigator who witnessed the explosive growth of our science in the past fifty years can afford to be dogmatic about its course in the immediate future, let alone about the direction in which it will ultimately take us. So rather than trying to guess, let us conclude this chapter with the sober words with which Edwin P. Hubble, the foremost student of distant galaxies in the first half of this century, concluded his book *Realm of the Nebulae* in 1936, and which still ring as true as they did when they were written:

'Thus the exploration of space ends on a note of uncertainty. And necessarily so. We are, by definition, in the very centre of the observable region. Our immediate neighbourhood we know rather intimately; but with increasing distance our knowledge begins to fade, and fades rapidly. Eventually, we reach the dim boundary— the utmost limits attainable with our telescopes. There, we measure shadows; and we search among ghostly errors of measurement for landmarks which are scarcely more substantial.

The quest will continue. But not until the empirical resources have been exhausted, need we pass on to the dreamy realms of speculation'.

7 Retrospects and Prospects

In the preceding six chapters of this little volume, aiming to sketch the gradual outgrowth of human views on cosmology, we accompanied the reader from the commencement of our story more than two thousand years ago to the present day; and from the distance of our almost legendary predecessors in the Hellenistic times to the front-lines of current research. In looking back at the scientific achievements of our predecessors, we wish now to emphasize one human aspect of our story which did not, perhaps, fully transpire from all our previous account: namely, the utter minuteness of the relative number of astronomers throughout the ages, to whom we owe all our knowledge.

How many people did take an active part in the development of our science at (say) the time of its efflorescence in the 3rd century B.C., or concerned themselves with it? Even at the peak of the scientific activity of the Hellenistic epoch, the number of those who were creatively active did not exceed a few dozen—even when allowance is made for those whose name and work may have perished in oblivion—and the number of persons passively concerned with the accumulation of knowledge and capable of comprehending it ran, perhaps, to a few hundred out of more than some 50 million inhabitants of the Mediterranean world and of the Near East at that time.

Therefore, if we say that, by the 3rd century B.C., the rotundity of the Earth was a 'known' fact, we mean that it was known to a few hundred people who had the requisite degree of curiosity, as well as the technical ability to comprehend arguments which, simple as they appear to us today, must have sounded quite esoteric at that time. In other words, the rotundity of the Earth was 'known' in the 3rd century B.C. in much the same fashion as (say) the general theory of relativity is 'known' in our own time—to a few hundred, perhaps, out of a million in the 'developed' countries; and much less among those who have failed so far to absorb the full extent of human civilization.

At the time of the Renaissance, the average 'man-in-the-street' began to be vaguely aware that the Earth might be a sphere. That is why the spiritual authorities of that day became concerned with its regulation. The existence of a 'flat-Earth Society' in Great Britain still today attests to a dispersion of this particular 'packet' of human thought, and to the time-span between the avant-garde and the backwash of this particular idea in the mainstream of history. It is perhaps fair to say that as large a fraction of the people deny the sphericity of the Earth as the proportion of those who believed in it 23 centuries ago.

At the time of the Hellenistic civilization, therefore, not more than about one man in a million had a justification to call himself a 'natural philosopher' in the astronomical sense, and this number has remained approximately the same for a very long time. At the dawn of modern astronomy, during the time of Kepler and Galileo, the number of professional astronomers (together with those who took part in the intellectual ferment of the time) did not exceed about fifty—the first edition of Kepler's *Astronomia Nova* found scarcely that many interested readers.

Following the time of Newton, the community of scientists who concerned themselves with astronomical problems began to grow at last (for astronomy was becoming a subject of practical importance, mainly in connection with navigation), but still at a very slow rate; so slow that when in 1921 astronomers all over the world organised themselves into the International Astronomical Union, its initial membership stood at 207 out of a world population of 1 500 000 000, and even this small number contained a certain percentage of mere astronomical office-holders. At the present time, barely fifty years later, the membership of the I.A.U. has risen to over 2800 (i.e., a fourteenfold increase while the total world population has increased to four milliards); and at present keeps increasing by about 10 per cent every three years—i.e., slightly faster than the world's human population; but not much.

These figures amply document that, throughout all historic times up to the present, astronomers have always constituted a very small band and, numerically, an utterly negligible fraction of the world's population—a fact which should fill us with all the greater admiration for what they have accomplished: to set the Earth in motion; to recognise the model of the solar system and measure its dimensions; to bridge by measurement the gap separating us from the stars; to recognise the structure of our Galaxy; to discover other galaxies and identify objects whose distance from us is expressed in a thousand million light years! All these contributions to our knowledge, made in the past two thousand years, moulded and permanently transformed the intellectual outlook of mankind. Surely in no other instance known to the cultural history of the human race did so few accomplish so much for so many—often at the risk to their livelihood, and sometimes to their lives!

Religions had, to be sure, at times brought about greater or more sudden upheavals. But these lacked permanence, resting as they did on foundations which came to be contested destructively by their successors, and eventually withered away. On the other hand, science has represented the only activity of the human mind whose effects have been truly cumulative, regardless of any barriers of time, race, or language.

If, next, we turn our minds to the future and to what it may hold in store for our endless quest, we should keep in mind that the interval of time during which we have been engaged in its pursuit has, on cosmic scales, been fleetingly short so far. Indeed, while the first fundamental astronomical discoveries about the motion of the Sun and the Moon may be a few thousand years old and ante-date written history, scientific cosmology as a systematic discipline has existed for barely more than two thousand years. In the course of this time, a gradual accumulation of knowledge brought about profound changes in our views on our own position in the Universe. In particular, at the commencement of our story, many parts of it, then incomprehensible to the human mind, were regarded as the work, or intervention, of divine beings whose images were largely conjured up for this purpose. In later times, certainly since the dawn of celestial mechanics in the 17th century, we witnessed these divinities reduced one by one to the role of constitutional monarchs, who may be kept in existence for reasons of decorum, but without any astronomical necessity or influence on the stars in their courses.

Moreover, the account of our subject in the preceding chapter of this book has made it clear that the most part of our knowledge of more distant parts of the Universe has been obtained in the past hundred, if not the past fifty years. And more important still, the current progress in our knowledge is proceeding at such breathtaking speed that it is virtually impossible to extrapolate its course too far in the future.

In an earlier part of this book we compared the gradual evolution of astronomy to a meandering river, which now and then becomes accelerated in rapids. In the past, such periods of acceleration were encountered, for example, at the time of the discovery of the telescope in 1610, or in the last part of the 18th century when William Herschel with the aid of his reflectors 'coelorum perrupit claustra'. At the present time, since 1960, we have perhaps entered the most torrential rapids ever encountered in astronomy, by our sudden acquisition of the ability to lift the instruments of astronomical observation beyond the confines of the terrestrial atmosphere into interplanetary space.

This advent of space astronomy, which current advances in rocket technology and communication engineering have so suddenly thrust upon us, bids fair to accomplish the greatest single expansion of our astronomical horizons witnessed so far, and so rapidly to relegate ground-based astronomical observations into obsolescence. The day is perhaps not far (astronomically speaking) when such proud seats of terrestrial astronomy as the Observatories of Paris, Greenwich, or Pulkovo will descend to the historical place of Tycho Brahe's Uraniborg or of the Samarkand Observatory of Ulugh Bek—with the main observational activities being carried out by instrumentation in orbits (or on the Moon).

What will this great expansion of our horizons which is now taking place reveal to our eyes is as yet impossible to foresee. But in order to gain perspective, let us keep in mind that while the human race on this planet is barely half a million years old (and the science of astronomy barely two thousand years), the cosmic as well as biological future of man on the Earth may extend for many millions of years. In other words, the biological career of the genus Homo Sapiens in the solar system (already not limited exclusively to the Earth) is at the very beginning, and intellectually it is still in early infancy. This thought should fill us with both humility and hope

—humility not to jump (in the manner of our religious ancestors) to conclusions in matters which we do not as yet comprehend— and hope (nay, a certainty) that problems not understood by us as yet will, in the fullness of time, be solved by our descendants beyond our most sanguine anticipations.

Should, by any kind of physical miracle, Aristarchos or Archimedes wake up after a time-lapse of two thousand years to join our scientific discussions today, only small vestiges of our present knowledge could be intelligible to them. But the current advance of scientific research proceeds at so fast a pace that should we ourselves be able to join in discussion with our descendants a thousand years from now, it is very doubtful if we could comprehend them at all. By that time, for instance, the manned exploration of space may be extended over at least part of the stellar universe around us; our individual longevity may be increased to centuries, and contact may be established with other civilizations within our galactic system. And in another hundred thousand, or ten million years?

But it is idle to pursue this speculation any further, for our crystal ball is completely impenetrable to a gaze into events removed so far from us in time. Great distances in time, like great depths of space, possess secrets which they guard jealously from the uninitiated, knowing that these constitute a part of their lure. Most of these secrets are as yet hidden from us, but we inwardly feel that their exploration is connected with the aim of human existence. By studying the Universe in space and time, we are contributing to a permanent and cumulative fund of knowledge as a bridge to the future. The ultimate aim of this journey is still concealed from us by an impenetrable veil; but this should only act as an incentive to us all to acquire more wisdom. And on this note of deep optimism, we wish now to bid our reader 'God Speed' on his own journey towards this goal.

GLOSSARY OF TECHNICAL TERMS

GLOSSARY OF TECHNICAL TERMS

Aberration

An apparent motion of the stars in the sky, due to the fact that our terrestrial observing platform moves around the Sun in the course of the year with a velocity which is about 10^{-5}th part of that with which the light of distant celestial objects travels through empty space. As a result, we have to 'aim' our telescopes at the stars in a direction which varies slightly in the course of the year.

Apex

An apparent point in the celestial sphere, indicating the direction to which our Sun with its family of planets is heading in space on account of its proper motion among the stars. The opposite point, the position of which indicates the direction from which we are receding, is referred to as the 'ant-apex'.

Astronomical Unit

Unit of length equal to the mean distance between the Sun and the Earth; it is equal to 149 597 892 km (92 955 642 mls), with an uncertainty of $\pm$ 5 km (3.1 mls).

Cannocchiale (or perspicill)

Early names given to the astronomical telescope by Galileo Galilei or Johannes Kepler in 1609 and 1610. The term telescope for this device seems to have been coined in 1611 by Galileo's friend Demisiani.

Cepheids

A class of regular variable stars called after their prototype of δ Cephei, exhibiting characteristic light curves with amplitudes of light changes of the order of one stellar magnitude; the variability occurs at post-Main Sequence stage of stellar evolution. Their periods are remarkably constant, and strongly correlated with absolute brightness ('period-luminosity relation'). The cepheids with periods of less than one day are frequently referred to as 'cluster-type variables', because of their occurrence in large numbers among stars of the globular clusters.

Cosmic Year

The period of revolution of the Sun around the galactic centre. It is equal to approximately 200 million years of our terrestrial time.

Deferent

An artificial geometric device to produce epicyclic planetary motions—an auxiliary circle with a centre moving along the basic circular orbit with uniform angular velocity. The planets were believed by the ancients (from Hipparchos to Copernicus) to be moving uniformly along many deferent circles piled on each other, to reconcile their observed nonuniform motion in the sky with the Pythagorean dogma that celestial bodies must represent a combination of motions which are uniform and circular.

Eclipsing Variables

Close pairs of stars revolving around their common centre of gravity, with orbital planes accidentally so oriented that, twice during each revolution, one star happens to eclipse a part (or whole) of the disc of its mate—thus giving rise to characteristic changes of light. Such systems are very numerous in the sky.

Ecliptic

An ancient name for the orbital plane of the Earth around the Sun.

Epicycle

An apparent motion of the planets in the sky, representing—in effect—a reflex of the motion in space of our terrestrial observing platform.

Equans

Or, more fully, 'punctum equans'—represents a fictitious point inside a circular orbit from which uniform planetary motion along a circle would be seen to exhibit the observed non-uniform angular velocity of orbital revolution.

Gnomon

An ancient instrument to measure the elevation of the Sun above the horizon from the length of a shadow cast by an upright rod (or a pillar).

Hubble's Law

Represents a dependence between the distance of an extra-galactic object and the red shift of its spectral line. Except possibly at very great distances from us, a relation between distance and red shift appears to be almost linear (Hubble's Law); and corresponds to a velocity of expansion of 100 km/sec (62 mls) per megaparsec.

Inner Metagalaxy

A local cluster of almost 20 galaxies of various types, within some 6 million parsecs around us (it may be a part of a large system, involving the Virgo cluster). Our own Milky Way, the Andromeda nebula (M 31) and that in the constellation of Triangulum (M 33) are the most important members of this group.

Isochronism

Of a pendulum—a fact implying that the period of oscillation depends (on any fixed point on the Earth) only on the length of the pendulum, and not (for small oscillations) on the amplitude of its motion.

Light Equation

An interval of time which light takes to traverse a periodically varying distance.

Light Year

A distance traversed by light in the course of one year. As the velocity of light is known to be 299 793 km/sec (186 282 mls), and the length of the year is 3.15569×10^7 seconds, one light-year equals 9.460×10^{12} kms or 0.3169 parsecs.

Magellanic Clouds

A pair of rather small galaxies of irregular type, visible to the naked eye in the southern sky (within $20°$ of the south pole), at a distance of 50–60 thousand parsecs from us. Both are members of the 'local group' of the galaxies around us (i.e., belong to the 'inner Metagalaxy').

Magnitude of a Star

A measure of the brightness of the object on a logarithmic scale, defined in such a way that a difference of one magnitude is equal to a ratio of 2.512 in their respective brightness. Absolute magnitude of a star is equal to its apparent brightness as seen from a standard distance of 10 parsecs.

Mile

An ancient unit of length, used throughout the ages and defined in various ways. Thus the Roman mile was equal to 1.488 km; the more recent 'statute' mile is defined as $1.609\,344$ km; while the 'nautical' mile used by seamen is equal to 1.852 km (i.e., one 5400th part of the terrestrial quadrant).

Novae

The term signifies temporary and recurrent flare-ups of dwarf stars at advanced evolutionary stages, during which the star in question may temporarily (in days to weeks) increase in brightness several thousand times. In spite of their spectacular nature, disturbances in stellar structure manifesting themselves as nova outburst are only ephemeral and skin-deep.

Nutation

A periodic oscillation in the orientation of the terrestrial axis of rotation in space, and due—like the precession—to lunisolar attraction on the equatorial bulge of the Earth.

Parallax (annual) of a Star

An apparent motion of the star in the sky due to the annual motion of our terrestrial observing platform around the Sun. The shape of this parallactic motion depends on the position of the star with respect to the orbital plane of the Earth (i.e., the ecliptic) —being circular at the pole of the ecliptic, rectilinear in its plane, and elliptical at intermediate latitudes. The observed amplitude of such parallactic displacements can then be used to triangulate the distance of the respective object from us in terms of the Sun–Earth distance taken as the unit.

Parallax spectroscopic (photometric)

Signifies the extent of an annual parallactic motion evaluated from a comparison between the (measured) apparent brightness of the respective celestial object and its absolute (intrinsic) brightness estimated from the observed spectral features (or otherwise) on the assumption that the intensity of a light source falls off with the square of its distance.

Parallax of the Sun

The angle (computed) at which the equatorial radius of the Earth would be seen from the distance of the Sun. It is now known (by radar ranging) to be equal to $8.''79417$.

Parsec

The unit of distance at which the annual parallax of the object would be equal to one second of arc; it is equal to 206 265 astronomical units or 3.262 light years.

Perihelion (or Aphelion)

A point of the (eccentric) orbital curves at which the planet in question comes nearest to (or farthest away from) the Sun.

Precession

A secular motion of the axis of rotation of an astronomical body in space. 'Precession of the Equinoxes' represents an apparent secular motion of all celestial bodies in the sky, as observed from the Earth, due to the fact that the position of the terrestrial equator rotates slowly in space with respect to an absolute frame of reference (a motion caused by lunisolar attraction on the equatorial bulge of the Earth).

Proper Motion of a Star

An apparent motion in the sky due to the star's own motion in space ('peculiar proper motion') as well as to the motion of our terrestrial observing station ('parallactic proper motion').

Quadrature

Is the position in which the Moon or a planet is said to be when the angular distance between the Sun and the respective celestial body, as seen from the Earth, is 90°. For the Moon, the 'quadratures' occur at the times of the first or last quarter. Unlike the outer planets (from Mars to Pluto), inner planets (Mercury and Venus) can never appear at quadratures; their *maximum elongations* from the Sun attain less than 48° for Venus, and 28° for Mercury.

Quasars

Acronym for 'quasi-stellar discrete radio sources'—enigmatic celestial objects in the sky identified by their radio emission. Some 200 such objects are known at the present time; and although their physical interpretation remains still largely uncertain, some of them may constitute the most distant objects (up to 10 milliard light years away from us) within the reach of our telescopes.

Stade

An ancient unit of length, equal (probably) to very close to 200 metres.

Schoenus

An Egyptian unit of length, probably equal to 0.525 of a metre (21 inches).

Supernovae

Optically spectacular phenomena representing explosions in deep interiors of certain groups of ageing stars, which result in a total dispersal of the star's mass into space—in the course of which a 'supernova' may for several days or weeks shine as brightly as an entire galaxy. While, in the case of a nova outburst, the star merely 'blows its lid off' (which it can do a great number of times), a supernova explosion signifies the final and irrevocable act of stellar suicide.

BIBLIOGRAPHY

No single book published so far in any language covers the entire field of the present little volume; and the sources to many of its parts are widely scattered in different books and scientific periodicals.

For Chapter 1 ('Astronomy of the Ancients') the best single source remains T. L. Heath's *Aristarchus of Samos, the ancient Copernicus; a History of Greek Astronomy to Aristarchus* (Oxford Univ. Press, 1913).

For Chapter 2 ('Decline and Renaissance') the best single general source is J. L. E. Dreyer's treatise on the *History of the Planetary Systems from Thales to Kepler* (Cambridge Univ. Press, 1906). As far as Copernicus is concerned, the reader desirous of learning more details than are contained in our little volume may be referred to an older biography by Leopold Prowe, *Nicolaus Copernicus* (two volumes, in German, published in Berlin in 1883–1884); and to a more modern work by Ernst Zinner, *Entstehung und Ausbreitung der Coppernicanischen Lehre* (Erlangen, 1943). Another outstanding recent work by Jeremi Wasiutynski, entitled *Kopernik, Tworca Novego Nieba* (Warsaw, 1938) is so far available only in the Polish language.

As regards Tycho Brahe, the standard biography is still J. L. E. Dreyer's *Tycho Brahe: a Picture of Scientific Life and Work in the 16th Century* (Edinburgh, 1890); a more recent work by John A. Gade, *The Life and Times of Tycho Brahe* (Princeton, 1947) is shorter and less comprehensive.

For Chapter 3 ('The New Astronomy') the principal source concerning Kepler's life and times remains Max Caspar's *Johannes Kepler* (Stuttgart, 1948; English translation by C. Doris Hellman, London and New York, 1959). An unorthodox but highly imaginative and valuable biography of Kepler has been included by Arthur Koestler as the principal part of his *Sleepwalkers* (London, 1959).

For Galileo Galilei, the best and most critical single source covering his life and times (at least up to 1616) is Emil Wohlwill's *Galilei und Sein Kampf für die Copernicanische Lehre* (Hamburg and Leipzig, 1909 and 1926). Of more modern works, the reader may consult with profit Giorgio di Santillana's *The Crime of Galileo* (Univ. of Chicago Press, 1955). As regards Newton, his best biography remains Louis Trenchard More's *Isaac Newton* (Cincinnati, 1934), which in 1962 became available in a Dover paperback edition.

The text of Chapters 4 and 6 is based on many sources; but for Chapter 5 covering the life and times of William Herschel, two particular texts can be recommended to the reader. The first is J. L. E. Dreyer's extensive introduction (107 pages) to Volume 1 of the *Scientific Papers of Sir William Herschel*, published by the Royal Society and the Royal Astronomical Society in London in 1912. The other is *The Herschel Chronicle*, by C. A. Lubbock (William Herschel's granddaughter), Cambridge Univ. Press, 1933.

INDEX